How to Trick Yourself Into Doing Things You Hate:

Use Psychology, Self-Discipline, and Neuroscience to Suffer Less

By Peter Hollins,

Author and Researcher at petehollins.com

Introduction

What are you really capable of?

Just how much could you achieve if you pushed yourself to max out every last bit of your potential?

How different would your life look if you found a way to consistently remove laziness, fear, and disorganization?

If you are looking for answers to any of the above questions, then this is the book for you. Perhaps you have a long-held ambition in mind right now, or perhaps your goal is less well-defined, but all you know is that you want to *do more*.

Whether you want to make advances in your personal or professional life, improve your health, way of thinking, daily habits, financial well-being, creativity, productivity, or a mix of all of these, this book is packed with practical exercises and prompts to help you develop the mindset most likely to help you succeed.

One big caveat before we begin: In these pages you will *not* find any magical secret knowledge or clever cheat codes for an easy life. Instead, this book is about one thing and one thing only—**the power of inspired and intentional action**.

Here is a statement that might surprise you: Reading this book will bring precisely zero benefit to your life. Yes, you read that right. That's because the words in this book do not hold any innate value in themselves. Rather, their value will only become apparent when activated—that is, put into practice by you, right now, in your actual life.

Because this is a book about the power of action, you will not derive any benefit unless you *actively apply* the principles shared here. Without action, this is just another book, and the information it shares is just that . . . information.

Learning to master the power of action allows you to access:

- more control and self-determination in your life

- more self-confidence and conviction in what you want to do
- greater clarity about the things you value and the things that *don't* warrant your attention
- more honesty about where you are right now, and realistic expectations about where you could be
- lowered levels of stress, and less avoidance, shame, and confusion
- more self-knowledge, awareness, and the ability to overcome self-limiting beliefs and procrastination

There are many more benefits to an action-oriented way of life and a mindset that favors growth, personal responsibility, and self-discipline. However, these additional benefits will be yours to unlock once you master the fundamentals of action in your own life.

Reading alone is not enough, and neither is insight or intellectual understanding. That's why with each new section, you will be prompted to take one small, concrete step in the right direction before moving on to the next.

If you've battled the demons of avoidance and procrastination, if you've fallen into patterns of "playing small," or if you're stuck in chaos, disorganization, and a lack of focus, then this book can help.

Before reading on, however, your first task is to identify that thing in your life right now that consciously or unconsciously inspired you to pick up this book—maybe you already know what this thing is!

Think carefully about the Big Scary Thing you've been avoiding, or the precious dream you've always yearned for but never had the courage to attempt. Perhaps you have a suspicion that you could do so much better in a particular area of life, or perhaps there is some unfulfilled possibility that you are finally ready to explore.

The ideas shared in this book are by no means easy . . . but they are simple. All you need is the willingness to learn, a little time every day to read and try out something new, and the hopeful expectation that **with effort, you can change**, no matter where you're starting from.

It's recommended that you keep a journal or notebook to jot down ideas as you proceed through each section. Not every concept will resonate with you, but a willingness to keep an open mind with new and unfamiliar concepts will guarantee that you learn something, one way or another.

Are you ready? In your journal, jot down the big goal you are hoping to make progress toward, and let's get started.

Chapter 1: The Real Meaning of Action

It all starts with mindset. If you are a person who deep down interprets change as a threat, perceives difficulty as a personal injustice, and views the outcomes of life as largely down to luck, you will tend to view life in a *passive* way. Your default will be to avoid action, to minimize effort, to shirk responsibility, and to face challenges with fear and resistance. Such a person might be able now and again to force themselves to act, but unless they address their self-sabotaging underlying mindset, the changes never stick, and like water settling at the lowest level, they eventually revert back to inaction.

The mindset that favors action, however, is completely different. Luckily for us, this mindset is not some rare innate quality that only some people are blessed with. Rather, it's a state of mind that we can intentionally cultivate in ourselves, starting right now. Let's take a closer look.

Develop a Bias for Action

In this section: Understanding what a "bias for action" is, why it's important, and how you can develop it.

Imagine two friends are having a drink together one day, when they start talking about how much fun it would be to create a podcast. They throw around a few crazy ideas, and soon both are feeling excited about the whole prospect.

"We should totally do this," says Friend A.

"Yeah, wouldn't it be great?" says Friend B.

Fast forward a week, and the friends meet again. Friend B is surprised to learn that Friend A has written a loose script and outline for the first episode, brainstormed a few names, investigated the right platform to host the podcast, and started listening to other similar podcasts for more ideas.

"So, when do you want to record the first one? What are you doing this Friday?" Friend A says.

"Hm, Friday will be tricky," says Friend B. "I mean, we *will* do it. This is an awesome idea, for sure, but there's just a lot going on right now. Just as soon as the kids are back at school, I'll sit down and take a look again. We'll need to make a nice plan . . ."

Can you see the big difference between Friend A and Friend B?

Fast forward a month or six months or a year, and Friend A may very well have launched a podcast already, made a success of it, and even moved on to something beyond it. Friend B, on the other hand, is still waiting for that perfect moment to start. He's still "planning." He'll get around to it, of course. Except, he doesn't.

Friend B was focused on all the things that stood in the way, all the reasons they couldn't start, and all the obstacles preventing forward motion. "We can't do a podcast because we don't have the right kind of microphones yet. Let me research a little more about microphones first, and then we'll start . . ."

But Friend A's bias went the other way: All he was focused on was **what could be done right now**. In other words, Friend A had a bias for action.

If you take a look at Amazon's job listings on their site, you'll see that one of their main work principles is precisely this "bias for action":

"Speed matters in business," says Amazon's hiring department. "Many decisions and actions are reversible and do not need extensive study. We value calculated risk-taking."

In other words, they have figured out that erring on the side of action almost always brings greatest rewards. You'll see the concept of action-orientation thrown around in marketing and business circles, but the truth is that it's so fundamental an idea that it applies to pretty much any human endeavor.

Let's be precise and give a definition. **A bias for action simply means that when given a choice, you choose action over inaction.**

That means choosing *not* to hang back, to "research," to mull things over, or to spend time on preparations. It means not waiting around for when you "have enough time" or for the stars to align (hint: this never happens, as you've probably already noticed).

A bias for action means that **your default is to act**.

For many people, inertia, laziness, fear, procrastination, self-doubt, endless debating and analyzing, second-guessing, "planning," and self-sabotage are the default. But for those with an action bias, taking a step forward is the thing that happens automatically, to the extent that it takes effort *not* to act.

Of course, planning matters. Mindlessly acting out without thought is definitely not what we're trying to achieve. But when everything is said and done, only one thing really matters, and it's *not* how well an idea has been planned out, or how nice a project is in theory.

Throughout this book we'll be exploring all the many different ways that people hang back, delay, or get in their own way, whether it's through fear, confusion, or just the momentum of plain old bad habit. The theme we will keep returning to is the necessity of cultivating whatever attitude we need to in order to **consistently choose action** over anything else. Not plan to take action, not think about future action, and not prepare for action . . . but simply act.

Let's be honest: Life is hard. It's busy, the really cool stuff can seem scary and unobtainable, and keeping your head above water can sometimes feel like an achievement in itself.

Luckily, a bias for action doesn't mean you have to become an instant productivity machine who smashes every goal they set for themselves. You don't have to become an overnight hero. In fact, your task is in many ways an *easier* one: Just do something. Take a step, even a small one, in the right direction, right now. That's all.

There will never be a perfect time.

There is no value in perfectionism.

Most decisions are reversible.

You can act right now, even though you're not 100 percent clear on the plan, you're not feeling ready, and you're not super excited about it. You can act, even if your plan is still fuzzy and your confidence a little shaky. In fact, you can *always* act, no matter what.

Do something small now, see where it lands you, and go from there. This is the essence of a bias for action. We no longer see action as some final outcome of a process, but rather the necessary first step of every process. **When in doubt, do.**

Instead of asking yourself about all the many reasons you can't or shouldn't act, focus instead on asking: **What thing can I do right now?** Counter-intuitively, this is often the lowest pressure, least anxiety-provoking state to be in.

And yet . . .

If taking action is such a good idea and so easy to do, then why don't we do it more often?

There are many answers to this question, but most of it comes down to anxiety. We feel like we don't yet know enough to act, we're afraid of the outcome, or we're worried there's a risk we haven't prepared for. We feel we don't have enough authority or clarity or ability to act.

In your own life right now, think of the task you are procrastinating and try to identify the nature of the anxiety behind it. Take note of the excuses you make for why you can't act— they'll give you a clue about your current mindset. Once you've identified this underlying fear, start considering some easy ways to begin shifting toward a bias for action instead.

The 37 Percent Rule

How do you really know if you've done enough research? This rule may help. The idea is that if you have one hundred options, ideas, or possibilities, surveying just thirty-seven of them will give you a thorough enough idea of what you're working with. After investigating thirty-seven of the one hundred paths forward, you should, in other words, be able to act without feeling like you've been too hasty and risked missing something important.

Another way to look at it is to imagine that you should spend just 37 percent of your time gathering and analyzing data, with the aim of acting as soon as possible. If you spend 100 percent of your time weighing up options, you'll get trapped and never do anything with your ever-increasing knowledge.

Gather Data, But Just Enough

One possible objection to the above: What if you don't know how much information is actually out there in the first place? Well, let go of the idea of getting "all the facts." It's impossible. Instead, focus on the crucial bits of information that you need, and then deliberately aim to be satisfied with 70 percent of that, and then act despite not knowing all the details. You will minimize risk while still being decisive.

Sure, gathering more data will make your decision better informed, but never forget that this comes at a cost—your time. While you're stuck gathering more and more data, you could have acted, failed, come back to the drawing board, and refined your position— perhaps many times over.

Create a Plan . . . After You've Broken Your Inertia

Set a roadmap of actions you will take and when, but don't get trapped in the planning phase. Break big goals down into smaller ones and keep each point on the journey focused on concrete things you can do. This is very different from aimless "research" that goes nowhere.

Keep coming back to the real world where there are specific steps you can take in the here and now. For example, make five phone calls a day, write five hundred words an hour, or turn up at the gym at least three times a week for a month. There is nothing wrong with planning, but keep it focused and practical. There's nothing to stop you from planning *and* acting.

Get Out of Your Head

One good trick is to literally count down to five, and when you get to one, act. Immediately. Don't overthink it, don't explain stuff to yourself, and don't give yourself a chance to come up with convoluted excuses. Just do the thing.

ACTION STEP: You've identified your goal, now set a timer for one minute and quickly brainstorm in your notebook as many ideas as you can for practical steps you can take toward your goal *today*. Small is okay. Just commit to taking that one step. Note how you feel once you've done so.

The Magic of Action-Oriented Decision-Making

In this section: An action bias doesn't guarantee success . . . but indecision _does_ guarantee failure.

Being able to make decisions quickly (decisiveness) is what separates the successful from the unsuccessful. It's not that acting decisively makes you successful; rather, it's that if you never act, you will never get the opportunity to win or to lose—it's as though you never played the game at all.

If success comes after a series of failures and adaptations, then the right strategy is to get started as quickly as possible getting those failures under your belt!

A bias for action saves you from the swamps of analysis paralysis (i.e., the illusion that we need to understand the entirety of all of the known universe before we can choose what to watch on Netflix). An action bias allows us to act more swiftly with less information and less angst and obsession. **The faster you fail, the more quickly you learn, and actively failing is always preferable to being stagnant.** However, when we're stuck in indecision, procrastination, and overthinking, we buy into the illusion that acting is the only thing that comes with risks and costs, while forgetting that *not* acting also comes with risks and costs, namely missed opportunities and wasted time.

Being overly hesitant or cautious may feel like a smart move in the moment, but drawn out for too long, it can end up reinforcing your underlying fear. The more you ruminate, the more confusing things seem to get; the more data you gather, the more you're convinced you don't know enough. Isn't it funny how that works?

Indecision quickly traps you in a weird no-man's land of inertia and passivity. You're not growing, you're not learning. You're not gaining resilience or experience, and you're not progressing.

Nowhere is this trap more evident than when we're faced with a decision. You need to choose which house to move into, which career path to take, which pitch to make to a client, which person to date, which meal to have for dinner, which vacation to take, which supplement to spend money on, which degree to study, or which name to call your new pet hamster . . .

Life is filled to the brim with choices and decisions. But no matter if it's work life or personal life, and no matter the size of the decision, you need a strategy. Mintzberg and

Westley (2001) explain the fact that so-called "rational" approaches to decision-making don't always work, and that there are other creative ways of engaging with problems and making decisions about them.

The "doing first" approach (versus "thinking first") is about taking action, noticing what works, then retaining the benefits before moving on. "Successful people know that when they are stuck, they must experiment. Thinking may drive doing, but doing just as surely drives thinking. We don't just think in order to act, we act in order to think," claim Mintzberg and Westley.

Thinking first may work well if the matter at hand is clear, simple, structured, and straightforward. But when you're dealing with a more complex decision that has many moving parts (like, ahem, life), or simply something you haven't dealt with before, it makes sense to go into "doing first" mode.

"Doing first" is what we default to if we are action-oriented people. Being action-oriented, we:

- overcome adversity with resilience
- stay focused and don't get distracted
- take charge easily and readily and are accountable for our choices

- embrace imperfection, challenge, and "failure"
- are curious and open-minded
- know how to be persistent
- find ways to be resourceful and creative, creating opportunities if we don't find them

A more "state-oriented" person, on the other hand (i.e., "think first"), will often be guided by fear; they will get distracted and discouraged by hypothetical "what-if" worries and focus on reasons something *can't* happen, rather than on all the things that *could*. They don't want the responsibility of choice and will resort to blame and excuse-making when an opportunity passes them by.

An action-oriented person feels regret when they don't act. When does a state-oriented person feel regret? The truth is, constantly. Lacking an action-bias means you feel remorse and anxiety before, during, and after a decision . . . if you ever get round to making one. Ultimately, **staying in the "comfort zone" is a trap**, as it's not really all that comfortable in the long run!

The "doing first" approach involves three processes:

1. Enactment
2. Selection

3. Retention

Essentially, you try out different things and "see what sticks." You take what works and run with it and leave behind what doesn't. This is nothing more than a process of ongoing refinement via real-world experimentation. Rather than standing back and worrying uselessly about the challenges you may encounter, you actively *engage* those obstacles and start chipping away at them. Every little action brings a small amount of clarity and a feeling of empowerment. You chisel away at the problem. If you don't act, however, the problem stays precisely the same size at it always was . . . or even gets bigger!

Enactment: Don't give inaction and inertia a chance to settle in. Take one small step in the right direction right now. The name of the game is active engagement.

Example: You're curious about setting up a small business selling your handmade soap. You immediately start experimenting with new recipes, make new batches, and hand out samples to friends and family to get their feedback. You're not merely planning to start a soap business—you've actually taken the very first tiny step toward building that business.

Selection: After taking a few actions, you stop and appraise the outcome. You get feedback.

You evaluate. Of course, not all of your actions will be 100 percent successes! But action-oriented people understand and expect this.

Example: You take note that everyone loves the shaped soaps, and that lavender is more popular than lemon. You also nail down a price that people seem comfortable paying, and get a clearer idea of who likes your soap and who isn't that interested.

Retention: Action has supplied you with valuable data about what works and what doesn't. Keep what works, lose what doesn't.

Example: You keep a notebook of recipes and fragrance formulations that have gotten the most positive feedback. Plus, you start experimenting with different lavender blends. All the while, you're taking new and further actions—perhaps chatting with small shop owners to see if they'll stock a few of your items.

ACTION STEP: In the last section, you took one small step toward your goal. That was enactment. Now, appraise the outcome you got, no matter how small. What good part of your results do you want to retain? See how you can repeat that today.

Understanding Motion Versus Action

In this section: How to get real about what *looks* like action . . . but isn't.

By this point, you may be wondering: How can you tell the difference between useful, intelligent planning and researching, and procrastination? Naturally, nobody is suggesting that you become a completely reckless person who acts without thinking. On the other hand, it can be difficult to know when you've crossed the line from careful planning into useless rumination and "going through the motions."

In this section, let's clear it up. Planning is a good thing. You need to plan. But sometimes, an activity masquerades as planning but is really just garden-variety fear, procrastination, laziness, and lack of focus.

One way to help you discern the difference is to think about motion versus action.

Motion is activity and movement.

Action is *focused* activity and movement that brings about *results* in the world.

We can also see this as the difference between "think first" and "do first."

To give an example, let's say you want to write a book. Motion is outlining and planning the book, daydreaming about plots and characters, attending a writing course, thinking about dialogue, jotting down notes, telling people your plans, and learning more about grammar and writing skills. You're "doing" a lot. But it's not *action*.

Action is, well . . . writing the book. Action is sitting down and putting one letter after another, one word after another, and building the book itself little by little. The difference is the *results*. Motion does not directly lead to results (although it has value in that it may indirectly lead to results).

Motion is necessary but not sufficient. Both motion and action matter. Typically, you start with the former, then move to the latter. What you *don't* want to do is get stuck on motion alone.

This is the illusory comfort zone where we fool ourselves and others that we're doing something when really, we're not. This place feels safe because we don't have to face our fear of acting.

The biggest illusion is that we are somehow being productive and moving forward, but at the end of the day, we have nothing to show for it. People who say, for instance, that they've "tried everything" are really saying that they've exhausted everything in motion mode but are now too fearful to move forward into action mode.

Of course we need to know how to plan, research, strategize, and carefully think about what we're doing. Action without motion is just as bad as motion without action. But if we're honest, most of us have to admit that our problem is not that we take too much action without planning, but that *we do not take enough action.*

The goal is to stay in motion mode only for as long as necessary. Here are some ways to do your due diligence in the planning-thinking-strategizing stage, but move on to real-world action as soon as possible:

Set Dedicated Times for Both

If you aren't intentional about it, you may find yourself defaulting to motion activities that ultimately go nowhere. Deliberately schedule the times you will spend planning, researching, etc., and times when you will be taking concrete, results-creating action. For example, block out 9 a.m. to 10 a.m. for writing but reserve the afternoon for planning, studying, or contemplating.

Microtasking

It's old advice but good advice: Break big projects down into smaller tasks. However, this breaking-down process is something you should do during your motion times. You want to be ready to simply dive into a pre-determined task when it's time for action.

For example, each afternoon you brainstorm, take notes and plan what you will sit down and write the following morning from 9 a.m. to 10 a.m. When 9 a.m. comes the next morning, you sit down and *immediately* start writing because you know exactly what you're working on that day.

Work Around Your Energy Levels

In our example, the action tasks are scheduled for the morning because this is the time you may be most energized, alert, and focused. Schedule your most intense and challenging tasks for when you're at peak energy, and book in the less demanding tasks in the time you have remaining. Even within a single scheduled block, you can budget your energy by doing the most difficult and important tasks first, then wind down with less intensive planning tasks.

Be Deliberate in the Shift from Motion to Action

Many amazing projects wither and die because the opportunity to shift into action mode comes and goes. The moment (and the momentum) is lost. You can guard against this by deliberately marking a point in your calendar where you will transition from planning into concrete action. At some point, research and theory need to stop, and the real work needs to begin—don't wait around for this moment to materialize on its own!

This step is especially true for bigger, more complicated projects. Choose a date to switch over and honor it, no excuses. Don't get too comfy in planning mode, no matter how many good excuses you can come up with to convince yourself otherwise! Choose a date and commit, then refuse to let yourself off the hook when the time comes to put plans into action.

In our example, this may mean giving yourself a month or two to carefully plan and plot your novel. But come D-day, you get to work writing no matter what.

A study in *The Journal of Personality and Social Psychology* (Gilovich and Medvec 1994) found that 76 percent of people don't regret the things they've done, but the things they didn't do. What do people end up regretting most? Basically all the times they chose to hang back in planning mode instead of taking the leap into action. Regret is nothing more than realizing that an opportunity for something great came and went without us maximizing on it while we could.

If you are having a hard time switching from motion into action, remind yourself that failure to do so is basically a perfect recipe for regret. Time is passing. Indecision, procrastination, and fear lead to inaction, and **inaction is guaranteed failure**, which can only lead to regret. The irony is that we may choose to avoid acting out of fear of failure, but in refusing to act, we guarantee that failure.

Don't be the person who is using ineffective busywork to conceal the fact that they are standing still. Don't allow intelligent planning and strategizing to stagnate and trap you in inertia.

If you're unsure whether you're truly acting or just keeping yourself busy, ask: **Does this activity lead directly toward results?** Does it bring me demonstrably closer to where I want to go? If not, be brave and take the leap. You've done enough planning. It's time for doing.

ACTION STEP: Today, set a goal for yourself in the near future where you will take a big leap toward the goal you have set for yourself.

Speed Versus Purpose

In this section: When it comes to productivity and success, don't think in

terms of speed or goals, but rather in terms of direction. Be purposeful first.

"Growth," says Dr. Scott Barry Kaufman, "is a direction, not a destination."

It seems like every motivational speaker and productivity guru in the world would disagree with Dr. Kaufman—aren't we all obsessed with how *fast* we reach our destination?

Speed may be your culture's measure of performance, but it doesn't have to be yours. Think about it: Is there any real value in working through a list of arbitrary tasks twice as fast? Is there any point in making loads of lightning-fast decisions if you're never sure *why* you're making those decisions at all, and to what end?

If you're thinking about doing the things you want to, it can never be about speed alone—unless, of course, your goal is to be a rat on a wheel whose main success is reaching burnout quicker than your competition.

To understand the difference between speed and purpose, consider a simple analogy: a car. The car's speed is just its speed; it doesn't tell you where the car is going or why. This quantity is called a "scalar"—it's a descriptor of magnitude alone. For example, "He drove at sixty miles an hour" or "He sold forty widgets."

Time and money are scalars, too. They're neutral, and don't "mean" anything.

However, a "vector" has both magnitude/size and direction. It's a car that is going sixty miles an hour *eastward*. This is a car that is driving to California. This is a car that is on its way to visit grandma for her birthday.

When we think about our actions, we need to **think in terms of vectors, not scalars**. In other words, it's not enough to simply assume that we will be more successful just because the magnitude of a certain measure is greater.

Consider in our car example that driving ninety miles an hour is not necessarily better than sixty. Why? Because if we were driving at ninety in the wrong direction, we wouldn't make it to grandma's house in time for her birthday.

In the same way, **we are not necessarily more productive if we work more hours, write more words, or sell more widgets**. That's because we could work long hours and learn nothing, write plenty on the wrong topic, or sell a bunch of widgets too cheaply, and ultimately make a loss.

Action matters, but not just any old action. Thinking of your actions in terms of vectors will keep you effective, focused, and purposeful. You simply cannot assume that increasing a scalar measure is a good indication of increased productivity or success. As Dr. Kaufman says, growth is all about facing the right direction. It's about making sure that the efforts you do make are being invested precisely where they should be.

So far, then, our goal is to be action-oriented and cultivate a bias for action (not just motion) that is *directional*.

How do we do that?

Think About Velocity and Not Just Speed

Velocity is speed with a direction. Think vector and not just scalar. This means constantly checking in with the overall trajectory and path of your actions, and the endpoint you're traveling toward.

- Are you learning and improving in any way? Is this growth?
- What is the wider impact of your choices and behavior?
- Are you going in the right direction?
- Regardless of your speed, is the quality of your actions what it should be?
- Ultimately, what does the action you're taking *mean*?

Reflect on Your Purpose

Having a goal is not the same thing as having a purpose. Many people set goals for themselves without thinking carefully about why they've set them that way. They direct their action toward this goal and feel that they are making progress (because, in a way, they are). It can be a rude awakening, however, to arrive at that goal and realize that it was not quite the right thing after all.

Losing a lot of weight, for example, is a goal that many people set for themselves. But *why* lose weight in the first place? The answer to this tells you about your purpose. Losing weight for its own sake is intrinsically meaningless. Losing it because your purpose is better health and well-being, the desire to live to see your children grow up, or the cultivation of the pride that comes with discipline and self-respect . . . these things speak more to purpose. Consider also:

- Do you have more than one purpose—i.e., are you actually being pulled in two opposing directions? What is the *priority*?
- In choosing what you want, have you considered what you are willing to sacrifice?
- Are your goals and ambitions yours, or have you inherited them from others?

Keep Tweaking the Trajectory

So, sheer speed or intensity alone are not markers of success; you need a direction and endpoint. And yet, not all endpoints (goals) are created equal. It's only those that connect meaningfully to a bigger purpose that will ultimately sustain you and guarantee real success.

But let's zoom out for a second. Realizing that you lack direction, purpose, or both is not the end of the world. Remember, we are not trying to be perfect or accomplish instant overnight success. Rather, our active decisions and choices always play out in small scale, day-to-day, ordinary ways. That means that if we discover that we are not on the right path (or not even on a path at all), we don't need to panic and assume that we have to abandon all our plans and start back at square one. After all, this all-or-nothing attitude may simply lead back to the impotent "research" mode where we get stuck dreaming up the next Plan B.

Instead of quantum leaps and grand transformations, try to think instead of eternal, tiny adjustments. Make a tweak, see what happens, make another. Repeat forever. You are more likely to reach your destination if you *keep moving* and make compound course corrections in the right direction than if you keep stopping and starting over.

Minor adjustments add up.

Have a Bias for (Small, Directional, Purposeful) Action

A person with a thousand unrelated goals achieves none of them. They divide and scatter their attention and effort and, though they appear to be very active, ultimately produce nothing and make no progress in any particular direction.

When we speak of having a bias for action, we do *not* mean a bias for mere motion and busywork, a bias for distraction and chaos, or a bias for setting "goals" that are more like pipe dreams and idle fantasies.

Many people now understand the necessity of having SMART goals but have not internalized *why* they need to set goals that are smart, measurable, attainable, realistic, and time bound.

Each factor is there to **ensure that your action and effort is purposeful, directional, and realistic**. It is a way to harness your abstract intentions and dreams into something concrete in the real world. It's one thing to say, "I want to make an extra one hundred thousand dollars." It's another to understand why you want that money, what you'll use it for, and every step on the path spanning the distance between zero dollars and one hundred thousand dollars.

Forget about how much you can accomplish and how fast you can accomplish it. Instead focus on the real value of what you are trying to accomplish, why, and perhaps most importantly, how.

ACTION STEP: Today, reflect on your purpose, your direction, and the ultimate meaning and point of your actions. A goal is not automatically a purpose! See if you can identify one step you can take today that feels meaningfully aligned with your purpose and not just your goal.

Put What You Read into Action

In this section: How to stop being a passive consumer of information and start actively applying what you learn.

So, preparing to take action, thinking about action, planning action, or intending action all have their place . . . but they can never replace action. Now, there is some irony to follow, given that you are reading a book about action, but the point stands: Reading about action is also not the same as taking action.

It may not be a flattering thing to admit about yourself, but try to **be honest about any**

tendency to use reading as an escape, avoidance, or delay tactic.

We've all known people who read voraciously, right? Perhaps you are one. Maybe you are in constant research mode, learning everything you can. Reading is a phenomenal lifelong habit, and the prestige that comes with being an avid reader is not unjustified. However, the gap between thinking and doing, between motion and action, can be especially wide when you read mountains of information and never apply any of it. This is especially noticeable when the content consumed is all about personal development.

You'll know that this is a problem for you if:

- You've read dozens of books this year already and have dozens more on your to-read list, but you'd find it hard to explain how any of these books made a practical difference to your life.
- You underline and highlight and dog ear pages but never return to these ideas no matter how fascinating you found them at the time.
- You often feel like you get an "inspiration high" from reading certain so-called life-changing books. But once that feeling fades, you're almost like an addict looking for the next fix . . .

Having an unchecked content addiction is not all that different from overthinking or procrastination. All these habits have different causes, but ultimately they amount to the same thing: a reluctance to act, to apply what is learned, and to make real-world use of new insights.

You may find that you become a genuine self-help and personal growth expert and "know" a lot, yet your actual life reflects none of this knowledge. There may be the illusion that reading allows you to "know" all about a topic and creates rewarding feelings of accomplishment and understanding. You feel like you actually possess the qualities, skills, and habits that you've read about, and may even look eagerly ahead to the next topic to investigate. But ultimately you are reading a book about minimalism instead of tidying your house, you are reading a book about communication instead of talking to people, and you are reading a book about productivity all while the hard work sits waiting for you, incomplete.

Be a Producer, Not Just a Consumer

Cherish what you learn by taking action that respects its value. Otherwise, what you have learned will only have the status of entertainment or distraction. Unless you apply the things you learn, they will be quickly forgotten. Unless they're embedded in concrete action, even the most priceless wisdom and knowledge will be reduced to mere data, something two-dimensional and arbitrary.

Forcing yourself to apply what you learn may slow you down, but if you engage with material meaningfully, you are so much more likely to derive genuine benefit. Look at it this way: It's better to read a single self-help book and truly apply its lessons for the rest of your life than to read two-dozen self-help books in the same amount of time and make zero changes to your life as a consequence.

Here are some ways to start making your reading and content consumption actually mean something:

Take Action-Oriented Notes

While you're reading, highlight or underline things that stand out to you, and jot down questions or comments in the margins . . . but don't stop there. When you're finished with the book, go back and re-read your notes. You can make a brief summary (let's say a single paragraph that captures the heart of the book's message) and then *generate two or three actionable steps you can take immediately.*

While you're synthesizing, summarizing, and revising material, constantly ask yourself in the back of your mind, "So what? What can I *do* with all this information? How does it fit in my life right now?"

Experiment

Even the most skilled and knowledgeable writer can only ever point to a certain idea or concept. It's quite a different thing to *experience* that concept for yourself. Imagine that self-help books are a little like travel guides. They're useful, but things really get interesting when you visit the place yourself and have your own adventure there, which is usually very different from the one the author had!

Create experiments where you test out the principles and ideas in the book. That way you not only test and confirm the wisdom on offer, but you also tailor it to your unique needs. You will never understand something as well as a lesson you teach yourself by real-life trial and error.

Try something new for thirty days, test out a new habit, or implement a certain bit of life advice and see what happens. You may even find that after doing your own experiments and reading the book a second time, you understand the ideas there in a much, much deeper way.

Stay Organized

If you read a lot and keep plenty of notes to help you stay engaged with the material, you may need a system to keep organized. Consider a master journal to keep track of other notebooks, a notecard system, or apps and software to keep track of your references, quotes, summaries, questions, and lists. Reading systems are as varied as the readers who use them—the best one for you is one that you design yourself out of experience and which serves your unique needs. You can also use a system like Goodreads to keep track of the books you've read, your ratings and reviews, and the key ideas you've learned from each.

Build a routine around reading. For example, set goals and intentions before starting, keep notes and make highlights as you read, log everything, and write a review when you're finished, and then immediately schedule in some actionable steps inspired by what you've read.

You might like to take a yearly approach, too, and review everything you've read each year, identifying the biggest gains, as well as the areas you're most interested in exploring next.

Join a Growth-Minded Book Club

One way to keep accountable and action-oriented is to read personal development books in a group. This way, you keep the material engaging and practical and bring the book to life by having conversations with others who share your interests and goals.

Friendly discussion can make the material mean so much more, expose you to different perspectives, encourage you to keep reading, and inspire you to implement the lessons. One thing you can do is actively encourage one another to share the ways you've applied lessons from the book, perhaps at the beginning of every meetup.

Be Mindful of Your Online Behavior

We will discuss the virtues of going on an "information diet" in a later section, but it's worth being alert to any bad habits that are keeping you distracted and addicted online. Mindless browsing distracts and demotivates you. Even if you do stumble on something of real value, you might just mindlessly scroll past it, completely unable to grasp the deeper meaning or retain its worth.

Instead, be more intentional about your online behavior. Before you sit in front of any screen, mentally tell yourself what you are about to do, why, and for how long. Set reminders or use productivity apps and blockers to set boundaries on exactly how you will spend your time and attention.

If you find something interesting, engage with it to completion before darting off to the next thing. If you can't (it's a long podcast, for instance), then bookmark it. Whenever next you find yourself wasting time online, remember your bookmarked list and return to some of your bookmarked material.

ACTION STEP: Take a moment now to review the five sections in chapter one. You may have liked and agreed with some ideas, while finding others less interesting or relevant. Pick an idea, sentence, concept, or suggestion that spoke to you most, and challenge yourself to put it into action somehow today.

Summary:

- It's important to develop a bias for action, which is a preferential focus on what can be done right now, rather than prioritizing abstract planning or thought. A bias for action means that when given a choice, we consistently choose action over inaction.
- There will never be a perfect time, there is no value in perfectionism, and most decisions are reversible. Ask, what thing can I do right now?

- An action bias doesn't guarantee success, but indecision does guarantee failure, and inaction comes with opportunity cost.
- A "doing first" approach allows you to act more swiftly with less information and less anxiety, then adjust and adapt. The faster you fail, the more quickly you learn. Experiment. We don't just think in order to act, we act in order to think. Act, observe the results, then repeat whatever worked.
- Action is not the same as motion. Sometimes, procrastination, laziness, and fear masquerade as action. Action is *focused* activity that brings real-world results. Motion is important, but be deliberate about moving on to action as quickly as possible.
- Likewise, don't think in terms of speed, but rather in terms of direction and purpose. Think vector rather than scalar when measuring your own progress. Being productive is not just about doing more.
- Don't be a passive consumer of information, but be a producer and put everything you read into action.

Chapter 2: What's Keeping You Stuck?

In the last chapter, we painted a clear picture of the action-oriented person and the uniquely effective way that they see the world. Hopefully, you are convinced that you should be such a person, that you want to be such a person, and that you can be that person. The good news is that by engaging with each action step, you are already on the path to becoming that person!

The trouble is, you might have also noticed that there are often things standing in your way. The best intentions seem to fizzle, procrastination creeps in, and you end up, one way or another, not acting.

Why?

The Causes of Inaction

In this section: How to identify the obstacles that are getting in the way of inspired action, and remove them.

In this chapter, we'll be taking a closer look at all the things that get in the way of what we know is the right path. Now, this isn't an invitation to lay blame, to feel sorry for ourselves, or to get trapped once more in passive overthinking. We are not here to find excuses for why being an effective, action-oriented person is simply not possible for us. Instead, the idea is that clearly understanding the obstacle empowers us to step around it.

Deep-seated procrastination habits and lifelong inaction can seem like complicated psychological phenomena, but really, there is no mystery. We fail to take action for one or more of the following reasons:

1. We hold limiting beliefs and have limiting thought patterns.

2. We feel fear and other negative emotions.

3. There are practical roadblocks.

Every human being will experience these three things in one way or another. This is important: You cannot learn, make a decision, create, achieve, or make changes without experiencing the above. Encountering roadblocks, then, is *not* a sign that you're doing something wrong or are on the wrong road. Let's consider each in turn:

Limiting Thoughts and Beliefs

These include all the ways your unconscious mind will jump in and try to convince you that change is a bad idea, scary, impossible, or not really desirable after all.

Whatever the action is, your self-limiting beliefs will tell you a story that results in you not taking action. For example, "I can't take action because . . ."

"I don't have enough time."

"Other people aren't doing what they should, and it's their fault."

"I'm just not that kind of person, and I can never be."

"It's too hard."

"I *will* do it . . . but later."

"I shouldn't have to change. It's not fair."

"If I take action, something bad will happen."

"I'm too young/old/tired/stupid/untalented/poor."

"It's unnecessary. I can get what I want without acting."

"Nothing ever changes anyway, so why bother?"

"Maybe I don't really want it after all."

And on and on. Your mind can come up with seemingly infinite reasons why you shouldn't act. None of them matter, however. It's normal to have this resistance, and it's perfectly possible to simply ignore it when it appears. Change is hard, and stepping outside your comfort zone is by definition uncomfortable.

What to do? Simply be aware and call these thoughts what they are: just thoughts. Not reality. Thank your mind for looking out for you, but realize that *you don't have to listen.* You don't have to argue with yourself or get lost in psychoanalysis, either. Acknowledge the thoughts with compassion, then take action anyway. There really is nothing more to it than that.

Fear and Other Negative Emotions

First things first: It's normal to feel fear when making a change or trying something new. In fact, this protective mechanism evolved over millennia and helped your ancient ancestors survive a threatening and unpredictable world.

Fear, then, is normal and even useful. Thankfully, we also possess rational thought, conscious intention, and free will.

Pay attention to what it is you're actually afraid of. Is it rejection, failure, or loss? Is it success and attention from others? Is it that achieving your goals would come with more pressure, expectations, and demands? Are we afraid of other people's judgments, or are we secretly worried that life will change in ways we don't actually want?

When it comes to fear, there is only one important thing to remember: It's not real. Fear is an electrochemical event in your brain. It *may* alert you to genuine danger in the world, but it's far more likely that the thing you're reacting to is a picture you've painted in your own mind. A fantasy.

To get a handle on fears, try writing them down in the following format:

"I want to (take XYZ action), but I'm scaring myself by imagining (XYZ fears about the outcome).

Take the time to complete the sentence above (a few times if necessary) to really drive home the fact that your fear is probably coming not from the situation itself, but from your imaginings about the situation. Pay attention to your thoughts, beliefs, assumptions, and unrealistic expectations and see if they are accurate. Is there any evidence that the feared outcome will really happen?

Here, too, small action steps and experiments will help release fear's hold on you. If you're afraid that people will judge you if you speak up with your ideas, conduct an experiment where you speak up in small ways, and observe—do people actually judge you as predicted?

Deliberately keep pulling your attention to the thing you sincerely want and the benefits of taking action in that direction. If you notice a distorted thought pop up, gently challenge it or ignore it.

Practical Obstacles and Roadblocks

Of course, sometimes there really is just something standing in your way. Challenges and difficult circumstances are a fact of life. Maybe you made a plan to fly somewhere but the flight was canceled. Maybe you want to learn to play the violin, but there are no teachers in your area. Maybe you committed to going to the gym, but you caught a bad case of food poisoning.

Do these things make action more difficult? Absolutely. But that doesn't mean we can't take action to overcome them. In fact, a person's response to adversity is often a bigger predictor of their ultimate success than their inborn talent or sheer luck. That's because if you give up at the first obstacle, it doesn't matter how talented or fortunate you are; at the same time, if you are willing to persist and push on, there isn't very much that can stop you, regardless of the luck or talent you started with.

Look around and identify people who have faced what you are facing, and get curious about exactly what they did to succeed. Carefully identify your skill or knowledge gaps and find a way to learn. If you're confused, ask for advice and help. If something isn't working, ask yourself what is working, and be willing to change tack. Realize that sometimes, an obstacle actually has a lesson to teach, if you engage it. What kind of a person do you need to be to overcome this obstacle? Find ways to take the first step to being that person right now.

The big message is that obstacles themselves are not a problem. Being action-oriented means not being afraid of obstacles or seeing them as a sign to give up. Rather:

- Ask precisely what it is that is stopping you from acting.

- Appraise that thought, fear, or feeling—is it real? Useful?
- Find a way to experiment with letting that thought, belief, or feeling go.
- Be realistic about your circumstances and limitations. There is power in honest appraisal of where you are. There is also inspiration in looking to those who have succeeded with all the same limitations that you currently have!

ACTION STEP: In your journal, make a note of what's really standing in your way. Answer some of the questions posed in this section, but go a step further: What small thing can you do right now to *directly challenge* your unhelpful thought, feeling, or practical circumstance? Clue: It will likely be the thing you least want to do!

Prioritize Action Over Motivation

In this section: Understand that action creates motivation, not the other way around.

One extremely common self-limiting belief is the idea that action comes from a feeling of enthusiasm, inspiration, or motivation. The corollary of this, then, is that we cannot or maybe should not act unless we feel completely inspired to do so. Sound familiar?

If you've ever said, "Ugh, but I just don't feel like it," and then delayed acting, chances are that you believe this idea too, on some level. Many of us are quietly waiting for something to happen before we start living the lives we want. We might wait for permission, for encouragement from others, for someone else to take charge and responsibility and *make* us do the things that are good for us. But really, the idea that action requires our joyful enthusiasm is arguably one of the most self-limiting beliefs out there.

The truth is actually the reverse: **Taking action creates momentum and enthusiasm to keep on taking action.**

If you make excitement and enjoyment a condition for acting, then you teach yourself to passively wait for better days and to instantly give up when things are a little challenging. It's a mindset that breeds procrastination, stagnation, and mediocrity.

We may start a new project filled with fire and energy, and when the fire burns away, we suddenly lose interest, or our excuses and justifications rear their heads and our impetus fizzles. It's a little like getting married and then losing interest in your spouse a few days after coming back from the honeymoon, because how could you still love them when you're no longer on vacation?

Motivation is better understood as a kind of momentum. It's like an engine on a cold winter's morning—it may take some effort to get it started, but once it's warm and running, it works easily and smoothly. Motivation is not a firecracker that gets you started on a new project with a bang; rather, it's a fire that you have to consistently maintain over time with small, everyday actions.

"Not feeling like it" simply has nothing to do with whether we act or not. When we are committed to taking action, we do it. That's all. And if we notice that our interest and energy is flagging, then all the more reason to take action, since it is only action that will get us moving again.

We act small, we experience the small reward of that action, and this encourages us to keep on acting, and so on. If we do nothing, however, the only thing that gets easier is to continue to do nothing. Getting started is always as hard as it is, and if we wait for some fabled time in the future when it will all somehow feel easier than it does now, then we could be stuck waiting a long time . . .

A common reason for people feeling "unmotivated" is an ironic one: They are actually expecting too much of themselves. They see the big picture of everything they have to do, and it's overwhelming. The solution is simple. Know that the big picture is there, but realize that **all you have to do right now is the very next step**. Just do today's work. In fact, just do the hour's work.

You may procrastinate if you keep telling yourself that you have to sit down and write a masterpiece novel. But that isn't really your task. Your task is only to sit down and produce five hundred words. In fact, it's easier than that: You just have to sit down and write *one* word. After you've done that, write another one. But there's no need to worry about that next word until you've written the one before it!

Think of it this way. Writer A may feel totally uninspired and decide they don't have it in them to write today, and so they don't. Writer B also feels unmotivated, but they sit down and write anyway. At the end of an hour's writing session, guess what? Writer B *still* feels a little unmotivated. The big difference, of course, is that Writer B has something to show for it—the five hundred words. The next day, Writer B has that little bit extra momentum because they are no longer starting from scratch. They find they can do 750 words this time. Writer A, still uninspired, watches cat videos on YouTube. There's no prize for guessing which of them will be closer to their goal in a year's time.

Try an "Action Ramp."

Pick a very quick and simple task that you can use to ease yourself into more difficult work. Let's say you challenge yourself to just quickly sit down and write free form for five minutes to get the ball rolling, after which you'll allow yourself to stop. Probably, after the five minutes is over and you're all warmed up, you'll discover that you want to keep going.

Try Mini Rewards

Taking action is intrinsically rewarding. You make an effort, and you can see the results. The world changes because of something you've done—what could feel more empowering than that? The great thing is that you can experience this satisfying feeling of reward even for small achievements. So, set yourself some mini goals and then give yourself a mini reward when you achieve them.

Reinterpret Your Feelings of Demotivation

Usually, we think that feeling uninspired, bored, or disinterested in our work is a sign to stop. Try to reframe this idea and see a lack of motivation as a symptom of inaction—a symptom that can be quickly relieved by doing something!

If you're having trouble acting, it's likely that you're overwhelmed or intimidated by your own thoughts about the task ahead (which is not the same as the task itself). Break things down and see if you can identify the very next step in the path, then just do that.

Make Starting Easy

Here's a useful trick: At the end of any kind of work session, try to leave yourself an outstanding task that will be easy and enjoyable to pick up when you return for the next work session. "Quit while you're ahead" rather than when you're in the depths of a particularly challenging portion of your work. You want it so that when you start up your next session, your first task is an enjoyable and easy win that will get the ball rolling. Try not to leave yourself with a stubborn challenge to work through as your first task, since this makes re-starting far more difficult than it needs to be.

Don't Let the Perfect Be the Enemy of the Good

You may set yourself the goal of, for example, running three miles every morning. But one morning, for whatever reason, you really can't imagine yourself doing even one mile. That's okay! Do one mile, then. If you can't imagine doing anything but walking half a mile, then do *that*.

It would be silly to say, "I can't manage a three-mile run" and then conclude that you'll do nothing. Instead, do what you can. No matter what happens, do something in the right direction, no matter how small. Make sure that no day is ever a "zero day." Wherever you are, whatever your circumstances, *you can act*. There's freedom and relief in that.

ACTION STEP: Decide for yourself today what the bare minimum is for you going forward. Make sure that you never have a "zero day" by identifying the smallest allowable action you will make no matter what. What does it feel like to make this kind of commitment to yourself?

Reduce Activation Energy

In this section: It takes energy and effort to get started—engineer your life so that starting is always as easy as possible.

There's truth in the old saying "Getting started is the hardest part."

In chemistry, "activation energy" refers to the smallest amount of energy necessary to trigger a chemical reaction. The analogy most often given is a person rolling a boulder up a hill. Once the boulder is at the very top of the hill and pushed just an inch over, it will roll down all by itself. Gravity takes over and no more effort is required. However, getting the boulder up to that point on the top of the hill in the first place *does* take energy—the energy it takes is akin to activation energy.

The principle doesn't just apply to chemistry, however, but to another "energy system" we might wish to trigger and sustain—that is, a certain behavior or action.

A general idea to keep in mind is the fact that **the greater the activation energy, the less likely a "reaction" (or for our purposes, a behavior) is to occur.** If our goals are overly ambitious, or the first step on a path is just too big to comfortably achieve, chances are we won't get that figurative boulder up the hill. In fact, we may waste far too much energy trying to roll the boulder up, and instead of having it go over, it keeps rolling down again. If your work has ever felt like an uphill battle, literally, chances are the activation energy of your chosen task is just too great.

We need to simplify, and we need to make things easier. We need to do whatever we can to lower that initial *mental* activation energy. Luckily, there are more than a few ways to do this. Of course, the hill is always there, and the only way to shift that boulder is to push it, but we don't need to make things harder for ourselves. Here are some ideas.

Don't Waste Time and Energy "Preparing"

Don't overcomplicate things. What do you *really* need to get a task started? Usually, it's a lot less than we tell ourselves. Getting carried away with unnecessary preparations is a great way to make that hill taller and steeper. For example, you don't need to buy an entirely brand new, color-coordinated wardrobe of workout gear and have a trainer-approved program designed for you before you're allowed to start exercising. Just get up and move. Take a walk or a jog. Go for a swim. There is very, very little effort required to pick one of the bazillion free online workout videos and get started right now, wearing nothing fancier than your pajamas!

Listen carefully for excuses about not being "ready" to start. You are ready! Often, the first step is not difficult, but we make it difficult for ourselves. Get moving *now*; you can buy workout gear later.

Break It Down

It's frequently repeated advice for a reason: It works. Break big tasks down into small tasks.

That way, you actually never have to do a big task at all. Just a series of little ones.

Don't fall into the trap of setting yourself ambitious goals, thinking they will motivate and inspire you. You may get an initial burst of enthusiasm, but that will quickly fade and give way to intimidation at the size of the hill in front of you. In almost every case, real success is made of many humble goals stacked onto one another; the grand, flashy goal *sounds* great, but often doesn't amount to anything in the end.

You can use the energy of a mini-goal already achieved to propel you into your next mini-goal. This is the rationale behind baby steps with frequent rewards. To use another analogy, it's a little like lining up dominoes, except the very first domino is tiny, the one after that is a little bigger, the one after that a little bigger still, and so on. Set up your goals right, and you can eventually topple the biggest domino at the end—and it won't *feel* like it required superhuman effort.

Find a Catalyst

In chemistry, a catalyst is something that lowers activation energy and makes a chemical reaction easier and more likely to occur. We'll have to work a little to make the metaphor work, but think in terms of anything that makes it easier for you to take those first few steps. Your goal here is to make the right action the easiest and most automatic habit— i.e., it almost takes effort *not* to take the action:

- Try "habit stacking," where you link a new desired habit onto the end of a pre-existing one that doesn't take any effort to enact (more on this later). For example, you effortlessly wake up every morning to go to the bathroom at 6 a.m. So, you place your running shoes at the bathroom door. Now, every morning at six, you go to the bathroom and immediately afterward put your running shoes on. Now you're out of bed and your shoes are on—suddenly it's much more likely that you'll go for that run you committed to.

- Enlist the help of an accountability buddy. Let's say they turn up at your house for that weekly study session whether you're "ready" or not. This simply gives you no option to procrastinate or flake out.

- Create an environment that shapes your behavior in the right ways. If you want to read more, then fill every room in the house with books and remove screens so that every time you're bored, there is literally nothing else to do but pick up a book and read. The environment is, in essence, acting as your catalyst, relieving some of the burden on your own willpower.

Cut Distractions

It's deadly to think of distractions themselves as rewards. We may allow interruptions to divert our attention, unconsciously thinking that it counts as a little "break." In fact, the opposite is true. All these little breaks are really like resets that bring the boulder right back to the start again. In other words, they increase activation energy and delay reaching the top of the hill, all the while wasting your time and draining your energy. Of course, you need to take breaks during your work. But the initial steps of a task are extremely important and vulnerable to distraction.

Don't switch from task to task or repeatedly reset your attention, or you ultimately make things harder for yourself. Try to get yourself over that hill as quickly as possible; the more you dawdle, the harder it gets. The sooner you get over the hump, the sooner you may find yourself in that easier, more flowing state of deep, productive work.

ACTION STEP: Look ahead to your next scheduled action. Find one way that you can make starting this action easier. Create a "ramp" or break things down so that the first step is extremely small and almost too easy *not* to do.

Overcoming the Illusion of Readiness

In this section: Stay out of the trap of waiting for "perfect conditions."

When it comes to action, the message is clear: Start now. Yes, right now.

Keep your ears pricked for all the plentiful excuses and rationalizations your brain will throw at you the moment you are about to get to work. These excuses will often sound like:

"I can't rush. I need to plan so I can do things properly."

"I'm not ready yet."

"I'll wait a little; it's not a good time right now."

"But I want it to be *perfect* . . ."

Of course, there is immense value in planning and conscious strategy. But let's be frank. That's not what these excuses are *really* about, right?

Previously, we explored one major misconception: that motivation is required for action.

In this section, we'll see some common variations on this theme, namely that we cannot act unless we are good enough, prepared enough, informed enough, confident enough, or skilled enough. There's some irony in this: We imagine that we are not allowed to improve until we're better. What a catch-22!

Procrastination is the most obvious sign that you may be "waiting" for the stars to align in this way. And it's a trap. You wait for the right time and delay action . . . but the right moment seems more distant than ever. It only feels less and less possible to act. Some of the worst forms of procrastination are those disguised as preparation and planning, as we've already seen.

Let's put it clearly: **Being ready is just an illusion. It's not a state you can ever meaningfully achieve.** Even if you do tick some boxes you believe are mandatory pre-requisites, the goalposts will move and something else will soon appear to convince you that you still cannot act.

When you find yourself wanting "more time," try to identify the fear underneath this excuse. You probably already know what you would do with this mythical extra time—waste it! Instead, start before you're ready. In fact, don't even bother appraising your readiness; it's irrelevant. If your skills or knowledge are not sufficient, then it's acting that will help you get better.

You don't have to see the very top of a staircase in order to take the first few steps on it; actually, there's no way to see the full staircase unless you commit to climbing it. **Anything worth doing is typically a process that unfolds with time.** That means that you will only know what it's like to be on that journey once you're on it.

There's no such thing as perfect, there's no such thing as ready, and there's no such thing as the "right time"—except perhaps the present, which is the only time we really have!

Even if there was such a thing as perfect, realize that your efforts don't have to be perfect to have value. If you're in process, by definition you *won't* be perfect. It won't be great at first, but moving through all the intervening stages is how you get to great. If you're a perfectionist, you don't allow yourself to be a beginner, and so you shut yourself off from the very experiences that would allow you to improve.

Perfectionists want to "skip ahead" and avoid what they see as the awkward and even humiliating learning curve. Try to turn this on its head: The messy, uncertain parts are precisely the place you develop your mastery and confidence. Expect mistakes and refuse to make them mean anything more than what they are: an inevitable part of the learning process.

If you're a lifelong procrastinator, your inner talk will automatically be at the ready with a million reasons why you can't act. *Acknowledge these thoughts and start anyway.* Do you feel unconfident, unsure, and nervous? That's fine. Take action. It's the only thing that will make you feel confident, sure, and relaxed.

An excellent way to get started (even when you don't feel like you're ready) is to create an "entry point."

Think now of all those tasks that have been lingering on your to-do list for a while. You know the ones: You keep putting them off and they keep hanging around, making you feel bad. Pick one of these and move through the following steps:

Step 1: Define the task as specifically as possible

Don't assume that this is obvious. Deliberately see how the task can be broken down into discrete subtasks. Think of the steps required in terms of manageable action. If you're having trouble doing this, see if you might need to break things down even further until it's really clear exactly what you have to do.

Step 2: Know what the first step is

Be clear also about the order in which you have to do these tasks, and line them up so that they form a logical progression, one to the other. Then, find out what the very first step is. If a task seems unclear or intimidating, keep refining and drilling down to what comes before it and what needs to be complete before you can successfully tackle it. You may need to adjust your starting point a few times—it's an iterative process.

Step 3: Find the entry point

You can think of an entry point as the specific thing you have to do to overcome your inertia and get moving again. It's the task that makes the rest of the process feel a lot less daunting. This is often the first step in the process, but it doesn't have to be. It may even be something that is quite insignificant in the grand scheme, but has value because it gets you moving. When you face resistance in the future, remember this entry point and aim for it directly.

When you are facing a large and complex task, your brain may try to convince you that it is too big, too scary, or too boring. You can really start to develop a mental block around the task, seeing it as impenetrable and unsolvable. If you find yourself with a "zombie" item on your to-do list that just won't die, it's time to ask:

"What is the first thing I need to do to get started here?"

You may need to then continue to ask, "But what about before that? And before *that*?"

By working backward this way, you chisel away at your apprehension and start to see a realistic way *in* to the task. Keep checking that your tasks are specific, practically defined, and manageable. They should feel simple, logically connected to the overall path, and easy enough to pick up right away.

For example, you might have a complicated insurance claim to file. It's been on your to-do list for weeks and makes you feel queasy just to look at.

Step 1: To define the task, you break it down into several minute subtasks (don't be afraid of making them *really* small, if necessary). For example, find the number to call, locate your policy, read the policy, decide exactly how you need to file the claim, etc.

Step 2: Once you've broken things down, you realize that a great first step is to find your policy documents, which will help you understand what to do next. This may even have a step prior to it—for example, digging around in a filing cabinet in the loft.

Step 3: You identify the entry point. You just need to get your hands on the documents and find the number to call, which will likely be on the documents. When you think about this step, it's so ridiculously easy that you can imagine doing it in a mere two minutes.

Simply starting has made the task seem suddenly so much smaller. In your mind, you needed to do four thousand things to file a claim. But by just starting and calling the insurance company, you've done half of the work already. This feeling of having to psyche yourself up for a big, complicated administrative task turned out to be nothing but an illusion. Within the hour, you have filed your claim and are surprised by how easy it really was.

ACTION STEP: Pick an annoying task that you have been dreading and avoiding, and apply the above process. Did the task take as long as you thought it would? Was it as arduous as predicted?

Developing a Victor Mindset

In this section: What a victim mindset is, how it undermines your efforts, and how to overcome it.

In this final section, we're going to be going a little deeper into a common psychological roadblock to effective action. We already know that faulty thought patterns have a lot to do with procrastination. There is, however, a broader and more pervasive mindset that sometimes accompanies inaction and procrastination.

Behind our more specific fears, thought patterns, excuses, and justifications lies a more deeply embedded core belief that we are, ultimately, victims of life in some way. By definition, it can be hard to own up to a victim mindset in ourselves because the first step is to acknowledge that it's something *we are doing* rather than something unfair that life has thrust on us.

Identifying and challenging unhelpful thoughts is great, but unless you can properly address the root of those thoughts, they will keep popping up again like weeds. If your overall mindset is one that resists and undermines action, then your work should not be at the level of individual thoughts and ideas, but rather the bigger core beliefs underneath them.

We won't delve into a detailed analysis of the victim mindset; it is enough merely to say that it's characterized by **the belief that one is, at the end of the day, not in control of one's own life**. Most of us can resort to a victim mindset now and again, but pay attention if the following has become a lasting *pattern* for you:

- You often blame other people or circumstances for your failures.
- You feel uniquely targeted by life, and that your experience has been especially unfair.
- You often find yourself waiting for other people's permission, approval, or validation. Sometimes you don't know what you think until you know other people's opinions.
- You sometimes feel better about yourself by identifying others who are doing worse than you!
- You secretly wish someone or something would come and save you, sort everything out, and relieve you of the burden of having to do it. You wish there was a shortcut or some secret hack to make things easier.
- Deep down, you think that others are more powerful and effective than you are.

- You don't feel very empowered or efficacious, and wonder if you were just "born that way" and can't really change.
- You hate failure and hard work, and maybe even feel that you're special in some way that exempts you from having to be uncomfortable.
- You sometimes feel sorry for yourself and devote a lot of time to exploring the "reasons" for your inaction.
- Rather than focusing on what you want, you're mostly guided by avoiding failure, rejection, criticism, or scrutiny.

Now, none of the above paints a very flattering portrait! But being realistic about our mindset is essential if we hope to change it and cultivate the better alternative: the "victor mindset."

The main difference is not that the victor is smarter, more talented, or luckier. Rather, **victors actively and consciously embrace their responsibility in life and maturely accept what they are in control of**. When things go wrong, they don't resort to blame and shame. When things are difficult, they don't assume that someone or something is being cruel to them. Ultimately, a victor does more because they have claimed their *agency and capacity* to do more. That's all.

How do we turn a victim mindset into a victor mindset?

Don't Compare, Contrast, or Compete

Victims tend to compare themselves (favorably or unfavorably) to others, letting external judgments dictate their self-worth (we'll explore *healthy* comparison in more detail later).

Instead, focus on yourself and your own values and ambitions. Refuse to let your confidence fluctuate according to the perceived superiority of others, and instead make yourself your own yardstick. Compare your progress to your own achievements from a week or month ago, for example, rather than dwelling on what's "normal" or what others are doing.

Think Differently About Failure

A victim mentality is what mindset expert Carol Dweck would call a "fixed mindset"—one that believes that growth and learning are not possible and that we can never really change. The corollary is that if we fail, that means we *are* failures. Such a core belief means we are reluctant to ever take the risk of making a mistake, and so we prevent our own learning.

Instead, be realistic. Expect and welcome failure as a purely practical part of life. In fact, try not to think of it as failure at all, but rather just data: information that helps you adjust and refine. Why waste time feeling bad about it when you can simply apply what it teaches you, improve, and move on?

If failure is a big deal for you, a great challenge is to push yourself to ask for (and gratefully receive) feedback. Pay attention to the fact that the world doesn't end just because you are seen to be imperfect! In fact, it can be quite liberating to laugh at yourself occasionally. Who said you had to get everything right?

Drop the Shame and Blame

Someone with a victim mentality may have fallen into the habit of blaming others for their inability to take action. The solution, however, is not to relentlessly blame *themselves* instead. Rather, forget about blame altogether. While you are hunting for someone who is at fault, you may be missing out on key lessons and insights that are right under your nose.

Whenever there is a victim, there has to be a perpetrator. If you want to break out of the victim mindset, then, you will also need to drop the desire to identify the "bad guy" in every situation—that includes not beating yourself up!

Rather than dwelling on failures with thoughts like, "What is wrong with me?" or "Why is life so unfair? Why are other people so awful?" instead ask questions that can help you identify concrete actions you can take. For example, "What happened and what can I do to be better next time? What have I learned here? What *did* work and how can I do more of that?"

ACTION STEP: Today, a very unusual and possibly scary task—deliberately choose a task that you know you will be bad at, and do it imperfectly. It can be small, but don't chicken out. Notice any triggered victim mentality in yourself. Constantly push your mind to ask the question, "What did I learn from that?"

Summary:

- You need to identify the deeper causes of inaction so that you can remove them. There are just three overall causes: limiting beliefs and thought patterns, fear and other negative emotions, and practical obstacles and challenges that get in the way. Resistance is normal but not a sign that you should give up.
- Fear is not real but is usually a result of your imaginings about the situation. Challenges exist, but a person's response to adversity is the real determiner of their success.

- Action creates motivation, not the other way around. Taking action creates momentum and enthusiasm to keep on taking action. Remember that all you have to do is the next step. Try action ramps and mini rewards to make it easier.
- It takes energy and effort to get started, but you make action more likely if you reduce the activation energy required to get the ball rolling. Make the first step easy and don't be overly ambitious. Break things down, don't waste too much time planning, don't overcomplicate things, incorporate behavioral catalysts, and be ruthless with cutting out distractions.
- Let go of the illusion that you will ever be "ready" and act right now, as you are. There's no such thing as perfect, no such thing as ready, and no such thing as the "right time." Be willing to be in process.
- Lose the victim mindset and see yourself as a responsible victor who is in control of their own life. Claim control of your life and be brave enough to learn from your mistakes.

Chapter 3: Staying the Path

Getting started is the hardest part— but it's not the only part. Understanding exactly how to identify and overcome inertia was the focus of the previous two chapters, but now we have to answer the question, how do we *maintain* our momentum once we have created it?

The answer is with **consistency—i.e., the ability to not just take action but keep on taking action again and again**. Doing so is impossible without consciously developed habits and the self-discipline required to sustain them. Let's dive in.

Three Types of Self-Discipline

In this section: Understanding the three types of self-discipline and how to use them to plan, react, and grow.

Before we go on, ask yourself carefully what your understanding of self-discipline actually is. We all know we need it, but do we really understand how it works and how to actually be a self-disciplined person?

Is self-discipline just the willingness to push through tedious monotony so that every day is identical, with each minute scheduled and accounted for? Or is discipline more like courage and determination, a bit like passion but wearing combat boots? Perhaps to you, self-discipline looks like something a monk does—i.e., it's utterly miserable and has something to do with waking up at 4 a.m. and endless meals featuring steamed broccoli.

Psychiatrist and author Phil Stutz has pondered this idea extensively and believes there's actually more than one type of self-discipline. He outlines three: structural, reactive, and expansive.

Structural Self-Discipline

The self-discipline to build yourself a structured and ordered day.

Examples: You wake up in the morning at a fixed time and start working your way through your hourly routine—you exercise, then do a few chores, then sit down and get to work, and your work hour itself is also structured and ordered. Anytime you consciously make a plan and follow it, you are putting your willpower in charge, and your time and effort is subsequently structured.

Such self-discipline is great—when it works, that is. You won't get far unless you make a considered plan beforehand, and you will also fail if you allow a dip in motivation to derail you (as discussed previously).

The value of structured self-discipline is, naturally, its structure. But that structure can become rigid and unforgiving. What about if there was an emergency and your chores took twenty minutes longer than you planned? The trick to working through this approach's downsides is to allow pre-made plans to occasionally give a little. If for some reason you need to make a few adjustments and concessions, do it. The structured plan is only the best-case scenario—just try again to meet that standard tomorrow.

Reactive Self-Discipline

The ability to make concessions as described above is exactly what characterizes the second type: *the self-discipline to respond well to the unexpected.*

With structure and order, we succeed by following an outline. In real life, however, there are many factors and events completely out of our control. Success also comes from being able to adjust, adapt, and improvise in the most effective way possible.

Example: Your gym accountability buddy has bailed on you, your laptop has broken, or your great-uncle is ill and needs your help. What now? No amount of discipline is going to change the plain facts of life and unexpected circumstances. Sometimes, people can be spectacularly disciplined, but the moment their planned structure falls away, it's as though they suddenly give themselves permission to abandon everything. Sometimes this may be followed by enthusiastically blaming the unexpected event and shrugging your shoulders: clearly it's just not practical or even possible to follow through in the way you really want to, right?

But there is a form of self-discipline that allows us to respond meaningfully and intelligently to life's surprises without compromising on our commitments and goals. We make space for the fact that there may be some variation in our path, and that we can happily accommodate minor setbacks.

Expansive Self-Discipline

Finally, the third type: *the self-discipline to deliberately push beyond your limitations and expand out of your comfort zone.*

Structural discipline keeps us tethered to the narrow path; reactive discipline helps us respond wisely to the unexpected; expansive discipline is about aspiration and growth— what *more* can you do?

Example: Let's say you have a goal to read one high-quality book per month for a whole year. One month, you read a book in about three weeks. You could stop there and tick the box, but why not start immediately on the next book? In fact, why not challenge yourself to go a little further than you originally set out to? Maybe you could aim for fifteen books this year, or perhaps you could commit yourself to reading more challenging books that you won't so easily finish!

Expansive self-discipline is about making sure that we are always positioning ourselves at the growing tip of experience, and not just "resting on our laurels." Lifting the same weight every day will not lead to muscle growth. We can think of it this way: If we are not growing, we are actually standing still. Expansive self-discipline is the continued effort to not just maintain but increase.

Now, there are other types of discipline, too: emotional discipline (the ability to self-regulate, to moderate social interactions, to know oneself), cognitive self-discipline (maintain attention and focus, know how to concentrate amidst distractions), impulse control and moderation, intellectual self-discipline (critical thinking, patience, intellectual honesty), financial discipline, domestic discipline (the ability to mindfully maintain a healthy environment), social discipline (drawing boundaries, observing obligations), physical discipline, even digital and informational discipline . . .

But as you can see, many of the above are more properly thought of as arenas in which we can demonstrate one of the three main types. A self-disciplined person, then, possesses all three types of self-discipline and knows when to lean on one more heavily than the other. A self-disciplined person is:

- Someone who can plan, structure, and order their day;
- adjust, adapt, and react intelligently when the unexpected happens; and
- continuously push themselves to do more and go further.

You may find that one of these types is easier for you than the other. You may also find that your goals and intentions require all three types. Whatever the case, it's worth having a deeper and richer understanding of exactly what self-discipline is and the different forms it can take.

This way, we will not get trapped in the boring sameness of a routine that never changes, and we won't succumb to all-or-nothing perfectionist thinking either. We will also never allow discipline itself to become a comfort zone that doesn't challenge or inspire us.

Discipline is **not** about squashing any sign of spontaneity or creativity. There is not automatically any virtue in being rigid, repetitive, and joyless. By all means plan a complex and sophisticated daily routine and stick to it religiously, but be prepared to respond intelligently when life throws a curveball and conditions for perfect action are no longer there. Many of us get stuck on the "create a routine" part of self-discipline, but being a mature and self-disciplined person is also about finding a flexible and realistic way of living in the world as we actually find it.

How Disciplined Are You in Each Area?

Ask yourself the following questions:

1. (Structural) What ordered plans can you make to move closer to your goals? What's the smallest specific action you can take every day? What about right now?

2. (Reactive) How will you respond when things don't go to plan? What are the potential challenges you might encounter, and how can you mitigate them? What "plan B" strategies can you put in place? What's the worst that could happen here?

3. (Expansive) What is your long-term vision? What will you do once you've mastered the current skill or achieved your current goal? What's the best thing that could happen here? Could you do more?

ACTION STEP: A self-disciplined person is "someone who can plan, structure, and order their day, adapt intelligently when the unexpected happens, and continuously push themselves to do more and go further." How well do you match this description? Which area is least developed in you, and what could you do to improve?

Become 1 Percent Better Each Day

In this section: Understanding the law of "compound effort," and why continuous improvement is better than overnight transformation.

There is a legend that goes like this:

An ancient Indian ruler had discovered the new game of chess and was so impressed with it that he summoned the creator in order to reward him. The king offered whatever the man wanted. The man asked to simply receive a grain of rice that day to represent one square on the chessboard. The next day, he said he'd return for double the amount of rice for the square after that, and so on, doubling the rice for every one of the sixty-four squares on the board.

The king thought nothing of it and agreed. The first day he gave the man a single grain of rice. The next day he gave him two. The third day it doubled to four grains, then eight, and so on. By the tenth square, they had reached about five hundred grains. By the twentieth square, though, it had reached 524,288 grains, and the king grew a little concerned. By square twenty-four it was more than eight million grains, and the king began to realize his error. By day thirty-six it was thirty-four billion grains, and by the end of the sixty-four days, *the final number was 18,446,744,073,709,551,615 grains of rice—a pile of rice as high as Mount Everest.*

You get the picture: Exponential curves can very quickly turn tiny amounts into enormous ones. What is true of rice is also true of effort.

Continuous improvement is the principle of making small improvements every single day so that over time, these improvements start to compound on one another, creating something that is not small at all. Even if we start with a single grain of rice, we can build on it. In our legend, the figures grew out of control because they were doubled each time, but the truth is that we can enjoy these compounding rewards just by being 1 percent better today than we were the day before. That's because every improvement builds on the one before it.

Small, consistent, and incremental change can ultimately achieve more than a single quantum leap. It may not be glamorous or look especially ambitious—but then again neither did the single grain of rice at the start of our story! By making slightly better decisions every day, maintaining what you've gained and building just a little more, you are guaranteeing real results.

We've already seen that self-discipline is not merely the willingness to grind away forever in a boring routine that never changes. With compounding effort, you are never doing the same thing each day—you are always doing something a little different, a little better each time.

The only thing stopping us from making use of this principle is our own mindset. We make many misconceptions. For example:

- Effort is only worth something if it is immediately followed by some big, flashy reward.
- Sudden and total transformations are more valuable than gradual changes over time.
- The process of achieving our goals should be exciting, noteworthy, even heroic.
- Small actions bring small rewards.

This last one in particular bears closer examination. **In the very short-term, there is actually not much difference between being 1 percent better, doing nothing, and being 1 percent worse**. Just looking at it, you could mistakenly think that there was no difference. But the difference takes time to manifest. A small action in the right direction *won't* impact you today—but that doesn't

93

mean it's not the best choice and that it won't impact you in the future.

According to Coach James Clear, if you improve 1 percent daily, then after a year you will be *almost thirty-eight times better than you are now.* And the great thing is, you will not have had to resort to drastic transformations anywhere to get there.

How can we use this principle in our own lives?

Find Out What Works and Do More of It

It's a mistake to think that you can only improve by finding some drastic new way to innovate or make a big, dramatic change. You can also improve by merely refining what you are already doing well. Focus on all those actions you have already taken and the habits you've already acquired and refine them. There is so, so much improvement to be gained by optimizing in these ordinary ways.

Avoid Small Losses

In the legend, the amount of rice never decreases. Try to do the same in your own life and avoid any tiny losses. Bank what you've done and protect it. While you are striving to continually make little improvements, also pay attention to minimizing mistakes and cutting out tiny inefficiencies. This approach, known as improvement by subtraction, is about the gains to be found in reducing errors, simplifying your process, and cutting out any unnecessary waste (we'll return to this concept later).

Measure Backward

Instead of just focusing on future goals and comparing yourself to them, measure your progress against past performance. This backward approach lets you make informed decisions based on actual data. So, if you lifted 100 pounds in the gym last week, then try to go for 105 pounds this week.

You may have an ultimate goal to lift a certain amount of weight, but it may be easier and more productive to simply think in terms of lifting a little more than you did before. This will help you stay focused and practical, avoid unhelpful comparisons to others, and keep you feeling motivated.

When you zoom in on the daily nuts and bolts of your routine and keep yourself focused on the ordinary and practical details of your discipline, you will find that the grander and more impressive goals will take care of themselves in time. This principle, in fact, is the focus of our next section.

ACTION STEP: Think about something you did yesterday that you thought worked well or that you're proud of. Can you find a way to repeat that action, only do *slightly* more of it today?

Process, Not Outcome

In this section: Outcome matters, but process is how you get there, so focus on what you can do today or tomorrow.

If you're reading this book, it's obvious that there is some outcome you've imagined that matters a great deal to you. None of us could live long or well without setting any meaningful goals for ourselves, but by now you're probably noticing a theme emerging: Even though we may be inspired by an endpoint we sincerely want, the only way to bring ourselves to that end point is to focus our actions and efforts in the here and now.

There is an unfortunate irony: In our haste to achieve our imagined goals, we can start to adopt a mindset and attitude that is perfectly the opposite of the one we need to actually achieve that goal. In other words, **being too "outcome-oriented" can hamper our ability to ever achieve that outcome**.

Does this mean we shouldn't set goals? Not at all! But we should be mindful of the kind of goals we set. Compare the following:

1. Lose ten pounds
2. Eat 1500 calories a day for two months

What's the difference between these two goals? The first is outcome-oriented, while the second is process-oriented—it's about the actions that we ourselves are in control of. Losing ten pounds is the finish line; it's the *what*, not the *how*. You cannot wake up one day and lose ten pounds. But you can wake up and eat 1500 calories that day. That is something you can do, and what's more, you can do it consistently.

We don't have direct control over outcomes. If we do have any control over them, it's indirectly via our daily actions and choices. You cannot make a publisher pick up your book, but you can write that book to the best of your ability. Every single day, you can take action and do the work.

Action-oriented goals keep you firmly in the realm of practical possibility. The irony, again, is that when we focus on process, not outcome, we are actually maximizing our chances of achieving the outcome!

The way forward is clear: **Set yourself goals, but keep them action-oriented. Commit to only those things that are genuinely in your control.** You may notice that this concept has some overlap with structural self-discipline. It can be enormously freeing and even fun to know that all you are responsible for doing each day is your pre-determined portion of the work. You don't have to achieve miracles in an afternoon. You are not worried about the "prize" at the end, because you have a smaller and simpler win right in front of you: Just do today's work.

Make goals actionable, keep your head down and focused, and the process starts coming to life one step at a time. Naturally, you don't forget about your master goal; it's just that you view this end point more as a guiding light that you occasionally check in with to make sure you're heading in the right direction.

Getting lost contemplating the finished outcome can give us a false and premature sense of accomplishment that then drains our motivation and leaves us feeling a little uninspired with the relatively boring steps it takes to get there. If you spend too long daydreaming about how awesome it will be to finish the race, you might discover that the actual running of the race seems so much less appealing!

The great thing about process goals is how eminently workable they are. You can measure them. You know when you've done them and when you haven't. And if you don't end up reaching your goal, you can look at the intervening steps and see how they could be changed and improved. For example, you may realize that closer to 1400 calories is what you need to aim for.

Start where you are, take action, then keep taking action, and build on what you accomplish in small, humble ways. If you're feeling lost and overwhelmed, a brilliant question that will bring you back down to earth is simply: "What small thing can I do right now to get me back on track?"

Outcome-oriented goals feel intuitively satisfying, and they may initially appear to motivate you, but they don't bring you any insight into how you actually get there— often, an outcome-oriented goal is indistinguishable from a pipedream or fantasy. When it comes to doing the actual work, you may even be demoralized by such a glittering dream of the future precisely because you're made more keenly aware of how much distance there is between where you are now and where you wish you could be. Typically, this will overwhelm and demoralize you. You may find yourself saying things like, "I know what I want, but I just can't see it happening for me," or even worse, "I guess it just wasn't meant to be."

When you notice yourself drifting into an outcome-oriented mindset, try to deliberately pull yourself back to the only thing you have real control over: your actions.

Prioritize the Process in the Present

The outcome is a single moment. Nothing more. But the process is a long-term, evolving, unfolding experience that invites your ongoing engagement. This is the place where you grow, learn, and improve. So, keep your attention *there*, where it matters.

Ask, "What are the small daily actions I can take that will build something bigger and take me where I want to go?"

Structure your daily habits and routines around these actions and do them no matter what. Keep your eye on the details. Plan your work ahead of time and then commit to only doing that. This could be getting in a fixed daily step count, making your way through a textbook or workbook, systematically tidying one room or area of your house at a time, or reading a chapter a day.

Focus on Concrete Action

Again, there is power in discrete, practical steps—the smaller you can break things down, the better. Writers can sometimes lose momentum because they are too hung up on outcomes. Instead, "focus on quantity, and the quality will take care of itself." Sure, the five hundred words you write might not be very good, but you have still succeeded in your goal, because your goal was to write. You have still honored your commitment and cultivated discipline. That's a win that can't be taken away from you. This approach could encourage you to write more the following day, where you just may find that you *do* write something good!

Embrace the Smaller Wins

We have all been taught that the big, glitzy achievement at the end of the road is what really matters, and everything that comes before it is just a boring slog, right? But it's not true!

The process may not be a very sexy one, but it is actually rewarding in more subtle and humble ways. If you stick to the plan you set yourself every day, that means that every completed day is an opportunity for a mini celebration. It's a great feeling: to know that you can do the things you set out to do and that you can enjoy every tiny step that brings you closer. Crossing the finish line is over in a moment, but the pleasure you get from learning to improve may be deeper and longer lasting.

The Art of Habit Stacking

In this section: How to make new habits from old.

If your aim is to take consistent, beneficial action every day, then you'll need to create a habit. A habit lowers activation energy, keeps you motivated, and leverages the power of compounded effort and incremental improvement. So far, so good. If you're thinking, "But making new habits is really hard," then think again.

A 2007 Oxford research study discovered that adult human brains actually had 41 percent *fewer* neurons than the brains of newborn babies (Abitz et al. 2007). This is quite a stunning result—don't adults know more than babies?

To understand the researcher's findings, we need to understand synaptic pruning, which is basically the process by which the brain gets rid of connections between neurons (synapses) that it no longer uses so that it can devote energy to building synapses that it will use. This is where the adage "use it or lose it" proves true!

The more you use a certain synaptic connection, the stronger it gets. The less you use it, the more likely it will disappear over time. Your brain is neuroplastic, which means that it adapts according to the skills it most needs to perform. It knows which skills those are because they're the ones you keep on doing. This is no analogy or metaphor here: The brain you have today is the one you built for yourself by repeatedly engaging in certain behaviors and habits.

Babies, not yet having cemented any particular habits or behaviors, have brains filled with potential. No pruning has taken place yet. They are like unshaped clay. The adult brains, however, have been pruned, and their shape is a reflection of their behavior, habits, and choices.

You may be wondering what any of this has to do with building new habits. The idea is this: Your brain builds itself according to your current behaviors. You already have habits, and their synaptic webs are already firmly embedded in your brain. Running through these habits is automatic and likely takes very little or no effort. You can take advantage of this fact by habit stacking—i.e., connecting new habits to old ones.

All you need to do is identify a habit you have currently and find a clever way to piggyback some new desired habit on top of it. The old automatic habit acts as a cue and trigger for the new one, making it more likely to happen and making it easier for you to build fresh neural connections with far less effort.

To make habit stacking easier and simpler, here's a formula you can use:

Say to yourself, **"Before/after/during [current habit], I will [new habit]."**

To give some examples:

"While I wait for my coffee to brew in the morning, I will do a quick body scan meditation."

"Before I brush my teeth every morning, I will do some mobility stretches."

"After I get home from work every day, I will immediately put my car keys in the dish by the front door."

"When I check my work emails in the morning, I will also check my calendar to see if there are any important meetings or deadlines coming up."

You can also use a simple conditional statement to treat one circumstance or behavior as a cue for another:

Say, **"If/when [X] occurs, then I will do [Y]."**

"When I write someone a birthday card, I immediately know I have to replace the card by buying another, ready for their next birthday."

"When the credits for a TV show roll, I know it's time to get up and do something else."

"When it's Tuesday and I hear the trash being collected outside, I take it as a cue to start sorting out the garbage cans in the house so they're ready for the following week."

As you can see, you are using the momentum and regularity of existing habits to bootstrap new ones. You are literally using pre-existing neural circuits in your brain to help you etch out new circuits. In time, the new behavior will also become automatic, but till then, you are leveraging the ease and automaticity of existing habits to keep going.

The fun really starts when you realize you can stack habits further—creating entire chains of behavior. As you have probably noticed, habit stacking also lowers activation energy and can counter that all-too-common trap of simply forgetting you had planned to do something.

As far as possible, try to stack habits in meaningful, logical ways so that moving from one behavior to the next genuinely feels seamless and effortless. For example, you take your vitamins every morning after you brush your teeth because the toothpaste and the vitamins are stored right beside one another in the bathroom cabinet. Think carefully about stacking habits according to proximity, but also keep them related temporally (in time) or thematically.

If you can teach yourself that one good habit is actually the trigger for another good habit, what you're doing is building high-momentum cascades of good behaviors that naturally link up to one another. Like the dominoes described earlier, however, **you only require the initial activation energy to kick the entire chain off**. You may not need complicated to-do lists and might only need to plan the structure once—then wind it up and let the routine play out! Here's how that may look:

"While I'm waiting for my coffee to brew, I do a quick body scan meditation. When the coffee is done, I stop meditating and go to my office, where I sit down and open my emails. Seeing the email inbox immediately reminds me to also open the calendar in another tab. I respond quickly to the easy messages and then check the calendar for anything important. This immediately triggers me to write/adjust my to-do list for the day. When my coffee is finished, I get up and go to the kitchen to get another one. While in the kitchen, I am reminded to feed the cat. The cat food is next to the shopping list, so as I sort out the food, I quickly check the shopping list to see if there's anything I need to add. If the list is big, I know that when I return to my office, I can amend my to-do list for the day to add *go to the supermarket . . .*"

As you can see, there is a blend of both structured and reactive self-discipline at play when we stack habits. If you do it right, it can actually feel jarring and uncomfortable to *not* do the tasks you set out to. You're going with the flow, and that can feel seamless and natural so that distractions don't seem to get as much purchase on your attention.

In time, stacked habits and deliberate triggers can start to form not just a daily routine, but a kind of deliberate, purposeful way to live. The "rules" you pre-determine for yourself can guide and shape your behavior:

"If there is a choice between stairs or elevators, I always take the stairs."

"Whenever I have a meal, I always fill half the plate with veggies."

"Should I get the urge to buy something new that costs more than fifty dollars, the rule is to wait twenty-four hours first."

Habit stacking works best when the triggers and cues are obvious and your response to them is a clearly actionable one. Make sure there is no room for delay or ambiguity. Remind yourself that as you build these intentional webs of behavior all around you, you are simultaneously shaping and pruning your actual brain!

ACTION STEP: In your journal, jot down a statement that follows either the "Before/after/during [current habit], I will [new habit]" format or the "If/when [X] occurs, then I will do [Y]" format. Could you commit to following through on this for three full days until the habit becomes automatic?

Gamify It!

In this section: To make habits more likely, make them more fun.

You can probably think of quite a few activities in your life right now that require zero willpower to start up. You don't have to talk yourself into them, you don't watch the clock while they're underway, and you certainly never "forget" to do them.

If the above immediately made you think of video or computer games, there's a good reason for that. These games have been designed specifically to catch and keep your attention, to spur your motivation to keep going, and to continually prod you to act. What you experience as "fun" is actually a deliberate characteristic of the game design.

In life, two things seem to be true:

1. You can understand that something is valuable and genuinely intend to do it . . . and then just not do it.
2. You can fully understand that something is *not* valuable and genuinely intend to avoid it . . . and still do it anyway.

We can call the gap between intellectually valuing something and actually taking steps to do that thing the "value-action gap." Caring about something, committing to it, and wanting it doesn't always translate into action. And yet, as any gaming addict knows, the opposite can also be true—we can understand how valueless an activity is and yet still be compelled to return to it again and again.

Understanding that this disparity exists is a necessary first step to doing something about it. We cannot reason logically with ourselves about the benefits of an action and assume that this alone will motivate us.

If your goal is to build new habits and stay motivated to do them day in and day out, you need to understand the value-action gap, as well as the different kinds of motivation:

Intrinsic motivation is a compulsion to act that comes from within you. You act because it's personally rewarding and because you're curious, passionate, or innately driven to value that action.

Extrinsic motivation comes from the environment outside of you. You act because you get a reward for acting, whether that's money, approval, validation, attention, perks, awards, promotions, titles, or prestige.

Sometimes, the value-action gap exists because we are relying too much on intrinsic motivation while ignoring all the ways we could prompt and encourage ourselves with rewards and achievements.

Gamifying our process is a way to build extrinsic motivation and mitigate the value-action gap. To gamify simply means to add game mechanics to non-game situations.

You already know what a game mechanic is: anything that makes you want to keep playing a game! This could include collectible tokens, milestones, prizes, "unlockable" hidden features, teasers, customizable avatars, leaderboards, performance tracking, upgrades, points, quests, challenges, badges, and plenty of friendly competition that keeps you hooked. In many ways, these features are difficult to distinguish from those that make gambling so alluring!

Gamification is merely a formalized way to engineer your external environment into a behavior modification tool. A game "trains" you by offering rewards (i.e., the feeling of fun and thrill) every time you get something right or perform the right action. Through reinforcement, you are taught to repeat the behavior. Thankfully, the behavioral techniques that game developers use to create genuinely scary levels of addiction to their games can be used in more benign ways in your own life. What could you achieve if you were as "addicted" to doing good things as you were to playing a game or gambling?

Game designers (as well as advertisers, activists, educators, politicians, and other social engineers) want to continually close the value-action gap on your behalf in order to compel certain behaviors. You can use their techniques to do the same in your own life so that the action you most want to do also happens to be the action that is genuinely most enjoyable and rewarding.

By incorporating game elements into your own life, you leverage both intrinsic and extrinsic motivation and exploit the fact that if you *want* to act, then you don't have to find the willpower to force yourself to do it. This can be especially useful for those with ADHD, who may thrive on novelty and challenge.

Break Things into Levels

This is more a mindset shift than an organizational one. You already know that it's wise to break big tasks down into small ones, but reconsider the name "task" itself. Think instead of arranging "quests" or "missions" or completing "levels." Doing a task sounds like a boring job, but completing a level feels more like a game. To keep your motivation up, make sure there is an appropriate reward marking the end of each level.

Make Your Own Reward System

The ~~tasks~~ levels you need to do will come with their own innate system of reward, but that doesn't mean you can't inject your own. For example, you may need to sit down and do your job day after day because rationally you understand that if you don't, you won't receive a paycheck at the end of the month and won't be able to afford food or rent. However, in the moment, this "reward" can feel very distant, abstract, and not particularly exciting. You might choose instead to create your own scaffold of rewards to motivate yourself on a smaller scale.

How you do this is up to you. Perhaps you could complete quests and missions to earn points or tokens and then use these to redeem for things you enjoy, like a coffee break, a treat at lunchtime, or simply a moment to say an affirmation that acknowledges your hard work. Not only will you be giving yourself a little dopamine hit that keeps you focused and motivated, but you'll be creating a way to track and monitor your progress at the same time.

Bring in a Little Competition

Too much of the wrong kind of pressure can demotivate and demoralize, but just the right kind in the right amounts can dial up the fun factor and encourage you to be more productive.

You could track your times and challenge yourself to a race. It's amazing how much you can do when you have *less* time to do it in! Try to continuously beat your own records, or even rope in someone else for a bit of friendly rivalry. Competition can keep your spirits up while encouraging you to continuously improve. It can turn optimization and challenge into a source of pleasure and even self-worth. You may discover that you actually feel energized after a prolonged and challenging bout of work, rather than depleted.

Remember that motivation and reward are extremely subjective and individual. Not everyone is motivated by the same things, and to the same degree. Nail down precisely what it is that makes you feel naturally and enjoyably motivated, and you can find creative ways to build that into everyday tasks.

A final caveat: Extrinsic motivation and gamified processes are great for those boring but necessary tasks, and for repetitive jobs that may feel a bit tedious day to day. It's a great way to essentially trick yourself into doing what you have already decided you must.

However, it's important that your overall longer-term goals have been mindfully chosen as things that are meaningful to you and that also motivate you intrinsically. There really is no point in hacking your motivation with game elements so you can be more productive toward a goal you genuinely don't care about!

ACTION STEP: Take a moment to think of the last time you were deeply absorbed in a task and ask exactly what it was that kept you hooked—was it the desire to complete everything thoroughly, was it the unfolding novelty and surprise, or was it the allure of besting someone else and being the winner? How can you build more of that into the actions you have to do each day?

Summary:

- Consistency is the ability to not just take action but keep on taking action over time. There are three types of discipline: structural (the self-discipline to build a structured and ordered day), reactive (the self-discipline to respond well to the unexpected), and expansive (the self-discipline to deliberately push beyond limitations). You ideally need all three.

- Continuous improvement and compound effort is better than overnight transformation. Aim to become just 1 percent better each day, and strive for incremental change that builds on itself. Find out what works and do more of it and avoid small losses.

- Outcome matters, but process is how you get there, so only focus on what you can do today or tomorrow. Being too "outcome-oriented" can hamper our ability to achieve

115

that outcome. Focus on process instead, and goals that are about consistent daily action.

- With habit stacking, you can make new habits out of old ones and make it easier to build new neural pathways with less effort. Habits make consistency possible, and you can build them by cleverly linking them to habits that you already have. Use the formula "Before/after/during [current habit], I will [new habit]."

- To make habits more likely, make them more fun and include gamification elements, such as competitions, badges, prizes, or levels. To close the values-action gap, make skillful use of both intrinsic and extrinsic motivation.

Chapter 4: It's Also About What You DON'T Do

If you have been following the prompts and action steps suggested in this book so far, then it's likely you have already discovered for yourself an important but often unappreciated aspect of the action mindset: that what you *don't* do can be just as important.

In a world of finite resources, limited time, and the genuine possibility of making a costly mistake on the wrong path, it's worth having good boundaries in place.

What isn't important?

What isn't necessary?

Legend says that when Michelangelo was asked how he managed to create the beautiful sculpture of David, he replied, "It's simple. I just removed everything that is NOT

David." This chapter is all about how we can apply the same principle in our own lives.

The "Don't-Do List"

In this section: Action matters, but sometimes the most important action is the one you don't take.

Even the most motivated and organized person can be derailed by distractions and irrelevancies. You may be very disciplined when it comes to doing all the right things, but are you also disciplined enough to say no to the wrong things?

Enter the "anti-to-do" list, which may be just the counterintuitive solution you need to stay more focused on what really matters day to day. If you're feeling perpetually haunted by a to-do list that never lets you rest, then try a "don't-do" list instead. Very simply, **this is a list of things that you won't and shouldn't do**.

Instead of crossing things off like you do with a conventional list, you make the list ahead of time, let's say weekly, and you use it to guide your upcoming days, making sure that you don't waste any time or energy on things you already know do not bring you closer to your goal.

What goes on such a list? That's up to you, but typically you'd include all the bad habits you're trying to quit, all the pointless diversions and distractions that eat up your precious time, and even those things that are useful and interesting but not necessarily *priorities* right now. We all know how important it is to have healthy boundaries; think of an anti-to-do list as a kind of **organizational boundary** that keeps you on the straight and narrow.

It takes a little time at first to identify exactly what behaviors and habits you need to exclude. To zoom in on precisely what to avoid, think carefully about the last time you had an ultra-productive and effective day, and compare it to one you felt was unfocused, confused, or unproductive. Examine your actual activities hour to hour and see if you can identify the habits that most reliably scattered your focus and drained your productivity.

Is it staying up an hour past bedtime scrolling on your phone in bed? Is it agreeing to have a long and unnecessary private phone call in the middle of a busy workday? Is it buying candy in bulk on the weekly grocery shop and then bingeing all that evening, giving yourself an enormous headache?

If you have already practiced habit stacking, you may find that some of the conditional statements you used also make excellent items for your anti-to-do list—for example, "When eating out, I never buy a drink" or "I never sit down in front of a screen unless I have a pre-determined plan for what I'm going to do."

Other examples:

- Don't work for more than an hour without taking a five-minute break.
- Don't watch more than one episode of a show on Netflix at a time.
- Don't drink more than two cups of coffee a day.
- Don't keep your smartphone by your bed.
- Don't go to bed after 11 p.m.
- Don't answer emails on a Sunday.
- Don't spend more than thirty minutes on social media a day.
- Don't work at home in pajamas (instead, get properly dressed).

There is a lot to be gained from simply *not* doing the wrong thing in life! All the above, for example, could be phrased in the positive ("take a break after every hour" or "get properly dressed when you're working from home"), but there is something about identifying what you *won't* do that feels more effortless. Psychologically, it doesn't feel like it takes any effort not to do something—and it doesn't. Yet the gains are still there. If you could improve your productivity, well-being, and enjoyment just by refusing to continue doing what isn't working, you instantly improve your life while saving energy and freeing up time.

What you don't do is important. **A bad habit can drastically influence your life just as much—or more than—a good habit.** Since we all have limited time and energy in a day, it makes sense to consider where we are currently wasting or mis-spending that time and energy.

That said, a don't-do list isn't sufficient in itself and isn't always appropriate. It's not a replacement for a proper list of tasks you will do, and it won't tell you how to use the focus and energy that you're saving. Also, a don't-do list will help you build awareness about the things that are holding you back, but you will still need discipline to actually refrain from doing them. Finally, a don't-do list is not set in stone and can and will change over time.

Step 1: Identify challenges

You may need to take a week or two to simply monitor your daily activities and see how you spend each and every hour. This can be an eye-opener! To identify those habits and behaviors that are undermining you most, pay attention to everything that comes *before* a feeling of procrastination, laziness, or demotivation.

Step 2: Make your list personalized, specific, and provisional

We've looked at some examples here, but your list will only serve you well if it's properly tailored to fit your life, goals, and distractions. Be as specific as possible, and focus on action—what are you specifically doing that is hindering your productivity? An item like "don't be so ungrateful all the time" is great but hard to quantify. "Don't complain" is more specific and actionable. Lastly, bear in mind that your list will likely change as your understanding of your own work patterns evolves.

Step 3: Check in frequently and challenge yourself

It may be easier at first to identify *just one* bad habit that you refuse to engage in during a given week. Pick the one that is having a disproportionately large impact on you, and start there.

However, in time, challenge yourself to add more items to the list while maintaining the momentum from previous items. You might like to revisit your list once a week and see what updates you can make. If you did something on the list, don't beat yourself up. Just ask why it happened and what changes you can make to prevent it from happening again.

Finally, try putting your list somewhere you can see it every day. You can gamify the process by giving yourself a small reward for making it through the week without doing a single thing from your to-do list. Celebrate the extra time, self-control, clarity, and peace it brings you. Spare a moment to think of something you genuinely do value and hold dear—how can you channel some of your saved time and energy into this thing instead?

ACTION STEP: Identify a moment in the preceding week where you felt yourself caught in procrastination. What happened immediately *before*? What triggered your avoidance, laziness, or forgetfulness? Right now, put a boundary or rule in place that makes it so that you don't engage that trigger again.

Progress by Subtraction

In this section: Ruthlessly cut away anything unimportant and keep focusing only on what brings results.

What is a "good life"? What does it mean, really, to live with discipline, purpose, and passion?

It can be difficult to define. In Christian theology, *via negativa* (Latin for "the negative way") is a path to understanding the nature of God by exploring all the things he isn't. In the same way, it can be a daunting task to try to figure out a good path for our own lives, but a much more manageable task to imagine what we *shouldn't* be and do.

The idea is to remove bad habits from your life, but it goes deeper than that. To put it in the words of Elon Musk, the goal is merely "**be less wrong**." If you continue to do so, you cannot help but eventually be right!

Progress by subtraction (as we've already explored somewhat with anti-to-do lists) is often easier because we can see more clearly what we are currently doing wrong. The "do more" mindset can be intimidating but also unclear—you might not even know what the right thing is because you've never done it before, right? So, all the positive affirmations, SMART goals, and pep talks rely on an underlying assumption that to be more, we must do more. But we can also increase goodness in our lives by simply removing what is wrong.

Remove distractions, temptations, obstacles, and wasteful bad habits, and the impetus to move forward in the right way will take care of itself—no supernatural willpower needed! For a simple example, consider the enormous number of productivity apps that exist out there today. You could waste your life researching new apps, installing them, figuring out how to use them, and devising complicated systems to organize your workflow ... or you could just sit down and do your work with pen and paper, forgetting about the internet entirely. Delete the apps, the six different YouTube videos explaining how to bullet journal, and the endless browser tabs with nine articles, blog posts, and eBooks explaining how to stay focused.

Another example: Instead of spending time and energy on building up self-esteem and other positive emotions, spend your effort on getting rid of the most damaging negative emotions you have right now. Instead of spending money on fancy protein powder and a gym membership, simply commit to quitting your post-dinner chocolate habit and train yourself not to keep junk food in the house.

If you're having trouble with procrastination, motivation, or distraction, ask yourself: **What can I get rid of here?**

In the book *Antifragile*, author Nassm Taleb explains that seeking first to reduce "downside" is a more effective way for people to become resilient and even thrive under adversity and challenge. According to Taleb, we need to systematically remove anything and everything that exposes us to risk, introduces uncertainty, or drains away resources. So, he would advise to prioritize getting rid of debt over increasing earning power, or quitting smoking and drinking well before you start fine-tuning the smaller details of your diet. Likewise, you may derive more well-being and benefit from removing toxic people from your life than finding ways to add relationships that are healthier.

Says Taleb, "In practice it is the negative that's used by the pros, those selected by evolution: Chess grandmasters usually win by not losing; people become rich by not going bust (particularly when others do); religions are mostly about interdicts; the learning of life is about what to avoid. You reduce most of your personal risks of accident thanks to a small number of measures."

Progress by subtraction is also easier! In real life, it can often be quite complicated to identify the right way forward or know which decisions to make. However, choosing *not to do something stupid* is always going to be the right move, and it's a move you can make even when you're unsure, pressed for time, or don't have all the facts. The negative way is also a subtle invitation to be more grateful in life. Pay attention, in other words, to all the bad things that could have happened but didn't, and all the ways that your current situation is actually rather good.

How do you apply *via negativa* to your own life?

Practice Strategic Negative Thinking

Who do you *not* want to be? What kind of life do you *not* want to live? What can you imagine being the worst possible outcome for yourself? Who inspires the opposite of envy and admiration in you? Start there and do whatever you can to avoid those things.

Eliminate the Stupid Things from Your Life

You probably already know what these things are. Time spent on stupefying and soul-deadening online activities, smoking, addictions, dangerous or illegal behavior, spending time with people who abuse or drain you, toxic food . . . Every one of us is guilty of something stupid now and then!

Be Ruthless in Your Priorities

If you have more than one priority, then you don't have any priorities. Take inspiration from the now famous anecdote about Warren Buffett, who asked an employee to list twenty of the things he cared about, then circle only three to focus on. The employee supposed that the things he didn't circle would come in second place, but Buffett corrected him: Those were the things he had to *deliberately avoid at all costs.* That's because sometimes the thing we need the most discipline to cut out of life is the good thing that gets in the way of the *great* thing.

Keep Your Eye on Action

Ask, "What can I remove or do less of that will help me take action more easily?" Your goal should be to remove anything that is getting in the way of you acting in the way you want to. That could be removing the option to enact certain habits (for example, making sure you don't have unhealthy snacks at home), or avoiding people, times, or situations that tend to make the right behavior more difficult.

Commit Your Freed Resources to Something Useful

By pruning away what you don't want or need, you will find yourself with freed up time, energy, or even money. However, nature abhors a vacuum, and if you remove a bad habit, you need to be careful that another equally bad one doesn't rush in to fill the gap.

Instead, deliberately commit any newly freed up resource to the goals you care about. For example, if you cut down on mindless screen time, use those extra hours every week for reading, exercise, or family time.

ACTION STEP: Asking, "What can I remove or do less of that will help me take action more easily?" can feel like a big question. An easier one to ask today may be, "What pointless or stupid thing did I do yesterday, and how can I make absolutely sure I don't do it again today?"

Go on an Information Diet

In this section: When it comes to information, be a conscious consumer and know where to draw the line.

"Content." It's what the online world runs on, and people everywhere feel irresistibly compelled to keep creating it . . . and keep consuming it.

But **information can be a drug**, and just as with other drugs, we can become addicted. When you wake up in the morning, you have a limited number of waking hours and a limited store of physical, emotional, and mental energy. Yet the online world *has no limits*; it is an infinite scroll of eternally refreshing "content" that only has one goal: to continually reach out and seize your attention and then hold on to it for as long as possible.

If your life is consistently filled with anxiety, overwhelm, confusion, stress, and high emotion, there's a good chance that you're simply online too much and exposing yourself to too much information. Could there really be such a thing as too much information? Yes!

It's only human to want to stay informed and in the loop, but without conscious discernment, we fail to pay attention to *what* we are consuming and *how much*. It's arguable that today most of us exist in artificial digital environments that influence us in more immediate, intense, and profound ways than anything we've encountered before.

We may encounter enough digital stimulus in a single afternoon to fill a year of life two hundred years ago. In the same way that our modern environment is obesogenic because it contains an overabundance of poor-quality food, our digital environment is conducive to mental illness because it contains an overabundance of poor-quality mental and sensory stimuli.

The old idea that one should stay connected because it is useful and important to know "what's going on in the world" just doesn't hold anymore; the information we are most frequently exposed to online is mindless and often worse than useless—it can be actively harmful. If we're honest, most of us have less control over our online behavior than we'd like.

If you want to reclaim your cognitive powers and sense of calm and well-being, if you want to think clearly and according to the ends and purposes you choose for yourself, then the solution is obvious: You need to drastically curtail the amount and type of information you expose yourself to. This can be thought of as an information diet.

Much-loved food writer Michael Pollan rose to prominence with his book *The Omnivore's Dilemma*, which eventually concluded that the ideal human diet was to "Eat (real) food. Not too much. Mostly plants." We can pattern our information diet on the same principles: **"Consume information, not too much, mostly facts."** Clay Johnson explains the plant-based analogy this way: "Eat low on the information food chain, and stick close to sources."

So, rather than reading a heavily biased article written about the point of view expressed in another heavily biased article, which in turn

131

was inspired by a handful of tweets and memes, just consult direct sources. For example, don't read analyses about a politician's speech—listen to it or read the transcript directly. Read official documents from court hearings, look up research papers, and fact-check as often as possible (nope, Wikipedia doesn't count!).

A proper information diet maximizes the useful and illuminating while minimizing the pointless or aggravating; you save time and spare yourself the enormous waste and disruption that comes from a lack of "online hygiene," but you also learn to become choosy about what you consume, opting for only the highest quality information and ignoring the noise.

It's the ultimate in *via negativa* and should probably be on the don't-do list of anyone living in the modern world. Here are a few more tips to forming a healthier relationship with the informational world around you:

Be Picky

You need to deliberately curate what you expose yourself to; don't wait for algorithms to decide what you should watch or read. Try as far as possible to never do a single thing online that you have not chosen to do on purpose. It is simply not true that if something is there, you need to engage with it.

To regain control and focus, decide ahead of time what informational channels you will pay attention to and which you simply won't entertain. You don't have to be on social media platforms, and if you are, you don't have to be on all of them. Pick and choose according to your values and goals. Try subscribing to newsletters or engage with more targeted long-form blogs, Substacks, and news sites. Routinely unsubscribe from anything that threatens to creep in before you've had a chance to decide its value in your life.

Go Offline Where Possible

Reading a book, magazine, or newspaper is a different experience to scrolling online. Invest in books (or borrow from the library) and refamiliarize yourself with real-world information sources. Pick things that don't allow you to speed up, skip ahead, or cheat with bite-size summaries and flashy but superficial titles. If focus is a problem for you, it may be worthwhile literally printing off pages and reading them away from a screen in a slower and more controlled way.

You could listen to quality podcasts, but don't multitask as you do so. Instead, sit quietly, eyes closed, and focus intently on what you're hearing. Occasionally pause to mentally "reply" to what you've heard so that you're actively engaging with the material and not just absorbing it passively.

Embrace Limits

Internet content has been *explicitly* designed to encourage unlimited consumption. It's made on purpose to be addictive. It's up to you to consciously moderate your intake, and that means actively choosing checks and boundaries. You could use certain tools and apps to block or filter certain topics or hashtags, and opt to receive fewer or no push notifications. Install an ad-blocker.

Informational boundaries also include moderating your own behavior, though. Set a time limit for a browsing session and literally get up and walk away when a pre-set timer goes off—no matter what. Schedule specific time blocks where you will engage with email, news, or social media, and refuse to engage outside those times. Identify particularly harmful, negative, or addictive content types/channels and eliminate them entirely— if something is toxic enough, the only safe thing is zero!

Be Mindful

One hallmark of overconsumption is how quickly we can lose conscious awareness of what we're doing. You will need to continually practice self-awareness and exert information self-discipline.

Whatever it is you're reading, watching, or listening to (that's online or offline), get into the habit of asking yourself:

- What am I actually doing here?
- Why am I taking this in?
- Is there any real value in this activity?
- Have I *chosen* this activity or simply drifted into it?

Often, we fool ourselves by calling certain things "entertainment" when, if we're honest, engaging with it leaves us feeling more bored, angry, apathetic, or aggravated than before. You may not even realize, for example, just how much a Netflix binge session is damaging your mood until you stop watching.

Go for the Good Stuff

It is not the mere fact that information can influence us that is a problem; the issue is that it can influence us without our conscious permission, and in negative ways. There is nothing wrong, of course, with consciously choosing to expose yourself to information that is uplifting, edifying, clarifying, or genuinely good for you.

If you notice yourself going down a rabbit hole or realize that you've wasted a few minutes (a few hours?) on something pointless, try to deliberately shift your attention to a "palate cleaner" such as an inspiring piece of music, a heartwarming video, or a funny skit that makes you smile. It turns out cat videos may be the best use of the internet after all!

Watch Your Action/Consumption Ratio

Finally, a good rule of thumb is to dedicate 20 percent of your time consuming content or information and 80 percent of your time *doing something* about it. This may take time to develop—just try to gradually shift the balance in the right direction.

One easy way to be more of a producer than a consumer is to write. Even a twenty-minute daily journaling session can powerfully shift your point of focus and allow you to start organizing, deepening, and expanding on *your own* thoughts rather than drowning in a never-ending flood of other people's ideas.

ACTION STEP: Today, try to notice any impulse or urge to jump online, scroll, or check social media. If you can stay mindful, pause in this moment and challenge yourself to address and fill any real needs you may have instead of going online. Are you actually tired, sad, lonely? Bored or procrastinating? What is going online helping you to avoid? Just sit for ten minutes and try to become aware of what your experience is when you're *not* covering it up with external stimuli.

Plan Ahead with Day Theming

In this section: What context-switching is, why it hurts your productivity, and what to do instead.

Most of us have been indoctrinated into the cult of the Sacred Hour. We plan our days in hour or half-hour chunks and may assume we need to switch tasks roughly once an hour. So, our schedules might list one hour on Task A, the following hour on Task B, another hour on Task C, and so on. We neatly cram in things like exercise, reading, rest, and planning the day ahead, and *voila*, we have the perfect productive day, right?

Except it doesn't always work out that way. What really happens is more like this: We sit down to do an hour of Task A. But before we can start, we need to get settled and into the right frame of mind. This takes the first five to ten minutes of the hour. At the end of the hour, we lose the final five to ten minutes distracted with wrapping up or planning for the upcoming Task B. When it comes down to it, we have not spent an hour on each task at all, but more like forty minutes—the rest is wasted on "buffering."

Every time you switch tasks, there is a "startup cost" in time, energy, and focus. You need to switch gears and adjust. Research from the University of California Irvine reveals that it takes an average of twenty-three minutes and fifteen seconds to refocus and get back into the groove of a new task—almost a quarter of an hour just to get going again! If you've ever felt like you've worked all day long and yet not achieved anything . . . then too-frequent context-switching may be to blame.

Getting rid of distractions and interruptions is one thing, but it's another to realize that there is a cost associated with simply changing tasks. Day theming is a technique that helps you minimize this cost and get the most value for the time you spend working each day. The idea is simple: **Switch tasks as little as possible. One obvious way to do this is to broadly stick with just one task per day.**

This doesn't necessarily mean you can only tackle one project or activity at a time—rather, you can group *similar activities* together so that you are not having to switch mental gears multiple times throughout the day. You devote each day to a theme, not a discrete task.

For example, you can devote Monday to writing tasks, Tuesday to errands you need to leave the house for, Wednesdays for research-heavy tasks, Thursdays for finance and other admin, Fridays for meetings, Saturdays for socializing, and Sundays for rest and recuperation.

Alternatively, you can plan your themed days a week in advance and organize yourself on the go, depending on changing demands and expectations. So, you may note down various practical errands in a list (shopping, in-person banking, collecting prescriptions, etc.), and then, when the list is long enough, devote a single day to doing them all in one go.

Day theming allows you to do deep, focused work on tasks without knowing in the back of your mind that you will soon need to stop and do something else. You become more efficient, more self-disciplined, and you may even experience less stress. You lower your activation energy and remove moments in the day when you're forced to regather your attention and willpower.

In some cases, you can even extend day theming to multiple days—for example, committing two or three days or even a week to working uninterrupted on a large project. Naturally, you will need to exercise a little discipline and boundary assertion to make sure that nothing and nobody is encroaching on the time you've dedicated to a task!

How to Start Implementing Day Theming

Step 1: Take stock of where you are

Where is your time currently going? More importantly, how many times in a day are you switching tasks?

One important thing to keep track of is all the *types* of activity that tend to fill a typical week. This will depend on your job, your lifestyle, and your goals. You might spread your time across tasks like phone calls, commuting, banking, emailing, report writing, and so on. Consider all these tasks and determine which are most essential, which could be eliminated, and which could be combined.

It's important to do this on the basis of real data and not just what you guess may be the case. Don't make assumptions; literally track your time for a week to see where it's actually going.

Step 2: Identify your overall themes

To theme your time, you will need a good idea of the main themes relevant to you. Again, this is not a grouping according to task but according to theme. For example, you may have several practical errands, all very different from one another, but they share the same theme of requiring you to get in your car and go into town to complete them. In the same way, you may be working on various projects for different customers. You may do all the finance-related tasks for all the projects on one day, all the communication tasks for all the projects on another day, and so on.

Once you've identified these themes, you can allocate specific days to each theme. You may set up a recurring weekly schedule this way, or you may decide to be more flexible and recreate the plan afresh every new week according to your needs. Make sure you're dedicating clear blocks of time for each theme, and mark the times in your calendar. Many people find large blocks of three hours ideal, with every hour containing a ten-minute break or so.

Step 3: Be mindful of your energy

There is no point scheduling hours and hours of deep work at a time of day when you're not energetic or focused. Plan activities to coincide with your most productive and alert times. You might reserve the morning for your most important tasks (like generating content, solving complex problems, or dealing with high-stakes meetings and negotiations), the afternoon for more routine things (like admin, organization, and planning), and the evening for easier, more relaxing tasks (reading, reflection, socializing, etc.).

Step 4: Assert your boundaries

Day theming is a task requiring structural self-discipline. Less discipline is required since you won't be context-switching as much, but you may require more discipline in order to ignore distractions and external requests to switch tasks. Interruptions are a part of life and not the end of the world, but if you want to protect and defend your hard-earned deep-work momentum, you can try:

- Clearly alerting colleagues and family when your work times are, and drawing clear physical boundaries. This could include, for example, a closed door, a do-not-disturb sign, or an agreement that when your headphones are on, you're not available.
- Install productivity apps and web browser blockers that block you from mindless browsing during your work sessions. Put your phone on silent or leave it in another room.

- Choose environments and locations that support long, uninterrupted work sessions. Go to a quiet library, for example, or set up your home office so that it is tidy, comfortable, well-lit, and quiet.

Before you've gotten used to day theming, it may feel like hard work; with a little practice, however, you may find that you never want to work in any other way. Day theming can make your life feel far simpler, less chaotic, and more enjoyable. It can be a huge relief in a hectic, hyper-distracted world.

Be the 1 Percent by Doing What the 99 Percent Doesn't Do

In this section: How to dedicate yourself to high-impact activities only.

By being someone who *does*, you are already streets ahead of someone who only thinks, feels, and plans. But by being someone who does *only the most impactful things*, you distinguish yourself even further and guarantee the best possible return on that effort.

Much productivity and self-help literature uses the word "leverage," but what does this actually mean? If we imagine a giant boulder and imagine how we can shift it by using a

143

plank and a small stone to create a *lever*, then we can understand the principle of using a tool that helps turn a small input into a large output.

Knowing exactly how to use mental, emotional, and behavioral levers is a way to maximize the energy and effort we have so that we are always achieving the highest possible impact.

Leverage is defined as the ratio of impact produced to time invested. Higher values come when we invest small amounts of time that yield large returns, accelerating our achievement. The converse is also true: There exist low-impact activities that cost enormous amounts of input and yield very little (we want to avoid those!).

In our quest to be more conscious, action-oriented, and focused, we need to learn to use certain psychological tools (akin to the plank and rock) to help us move the biggest boulders possible. As we've seen, doing 10 percent or even 1 percent better eventually adds up.

But where do you start? Here are some potentially insightful questions to ask yourself before you take any action:

- What if this was simpler?

- What if this was bigger?

- What else could I be doing instead of this?

By asking the first question, you are finding ways to save time and mental effort; by asking the second, you are finding ways to create more value; by asking the third, you are identifying possible opportunity costs.

Exactly what counts as a high-impact or leverage task will depend on you and your situation; but the defining characteristic is that you **amplify your effort**. This doesn't have to be complicated—simply automating certain tasks, delegating or prioritizing only the most impactful professional relationships, can get you disproportionate results.

George Soros tells us, "It is much easier to put existing resources to better use than to develop resources where they do not exist."

Optimizing your high-leverage tasks isn't about magically creating more time or spending more energy; it's about *strategic resource allocation* to create more meaningful outcomes, and that goes beyond a simple boost in productivity. Here are some ideas for exactly how you can do that.

Step 1: Start by tracking

You can't optimize your actions unless you know precisely what your actions are. Document and monitor exactly how you spend your time, energy, money, or other resources. Do this for about a week so you can really see where you may be wasteful, over- or under-investing, or else unaware of the true cost of certain tasks. Don't rely on perception or guesswork alone; be realistic also about the results you're currently getting and find a way to track your impact concretely.

Step 2: Pick tasks that fit your skill set

Identify those activities that best align with your abilities, interests, opportunities, and experience. Even better if you can zoom in on something that only you can do effectively by virtue of who you are. These are your naturally high-value skills and should be your focus.

Step 3: Set up your levers

Knowing what you're good at, move on and select activities that promise to deliver the greatest results for the time, energy, and money you invest in them. That may mean delegating something you're not so skilled at so you have more time to devote to the things you are, automating recurring tasks, or hiring someone else to tackle complicated work on your behalf.

The Pareto Principle

The Pareto principle is named after Italian economist Vilfredo Pareto and describes a theory he developed during the late nineteenth century based on the observation that approximately 80 percent of Italy's land was owned by just 20 percent of the population. Although the principle has many incarnations and originally had little to do with personal productivity, Pareto himself broadly believed that in nature, a relatively small portion of all causes was responsible for the bulk of observable results. To put it another way: Outcomes are often disproportionately influenced by just a few inputs.

It's the lever principle again! It follows that if we want to have the greatest impact while saving as much effort and energy as possible, then we need to identify that crucial 20 percent and apply ourselves there. Of course, in real life there is no precise mathematical way to identify the 20 percent. The principle is just a rough guide, but it's worth your while to pinpoint exactly those activities and targets that, if acted upon, will give you the most bang for your buck.

Working hard is great, as is finding ways to be more disciplined, effective, and productive. That said, you can work precisely the same amount but achieve more simply by being careful about where you spend your effort and how.

Where the Pareto Principle Doesn't Work, Try "Half-Assing" It

Very occasionally, you don't need to identify the most important 20 percent, especially if trying to do so makes you procrastinate even more. The perfectionist in you will resist the idea of doing a less-than-perfect job, but this could very well be the key to real effectiveness.

It may sound crazy but yes—*deliberately* do tasks a little poorly, carelessly, or incompletely. Why? Because if you do, then guess what—you've already broken through the inertia of procrastination, and you're already gathering loads of useful data about everything you shouldn't do in round two.

Just start, and don't let the fear of doing badly stop you—just accept you'll do it badly, then! Value progress over perfection. Even if you mess up royally, you'll have learned something, and you'll at least be moving. Even the tiniest step forward can start to generate some good momentum and feelings of reward that encourage you to keep going.

How do you half-ass things? If you have writer's block, for example, just sit down and deliberately write garbage with loads of spelling and grammar errors and all the cliches and stylistic errors you can think of (here we have the subtraction principle again—what happens if you return to this draft later and just . . . do the opposite?). Some people live in desperately dirty and untidy homes because, counterintuitively, they have such high standards that they don't even know where to start cleaning. So, they never start.

But if you deliberately half-ass it, then just agree with yourself that you'll start cleaning, anywhere, in any old way, without thinking too hard about it. Maybe you randomly pick an area in your home that gets seen most often by guests and cheat a little by cleaning only that.

Take shortcuts and rush a little. You don't need a foolproof plan and a new de-cluttering book and a clever strategy and a free Saturday morning. Just half-ass it. You may find that once you've started, the plan begins to emerge, and you feel more and more inspired to do a proper (not perfect) job. By initially intending to half-ass things, you paradoxically get a lot more done! In your case, the most impactful 20 percent was whatever you needed to do to get started.

ACTION STEPS: Look back at the past chapter and see if you can pick out the most effective 20 percent, or the idea that, if followed, would yield 80 percent of your success. Give yourself permission to ignore everything else! Double-check your goals or to-do list and see if, in light of this 20 percent, you'd like to trim away a few things that are just not as essential.

Summary:

- Action matters, but sometimes the most important action is the one you don't take. Compile a weekly don't-do list of bad habits, pointless diversions and distractions, and everything that is not a real priority.
- Progress by subtraction means we ruthlessly cut away anything unimportant and keep focusing only on what brings results. Be less wrong and remove distractions, temptations, obstacles, and wasteful bad habits.
- Information and content can be a drug; we need to be conscious consumers of what we take in. An information diet lets you regain control of your mental health, time, and attention. Be choosier.
- Context-switching or multitasking damages productivity and wastes time and energy. Combat it with pre-planned day theming so you switch tasks as little as possible. Group tasks thematically and aim for deep, uninterrupted work sessions.
- Consciously dedicate yourself to high-impact activities only. Use the Pareto principle to identify the most impactful 20 percent of any task or project, and focus

your attention on that. Leverage is the ratio of impact produced to time invested. Leverage your effort by choosing things that have as high a return as possible. Be strategic in how you allocate your resources.

Chapter 5: Zoom Out

In our final chapter, we're going to attempt to pull together all the threads we've woven so far. We've learned that consistent and purposeful action is what makes the difference, and that our success also heavily depends on what we don't do and how we respond to disruptions, obstacles, and setbacks. Now, we will take a step back and consider a few more techniques and approaches that can help you gain a broader, more top-down view of a sustainable, action-oriented life.

Cultivating Intentional Curiosity

In this section: How to reclaim mastery over your attentional field and harness your natural inquisitiveness rather than allowing it to enslave you.

Mental self-discipline can be a hard sell for people; it can feel like a loss of freedom and a boring thing that's all about constricting one's attention. Basically, it's no fun. The task you're tethered to can feel tiring and predictable so that when a distraction pops into your awareness, it takes on all the glamor and appeal of a genuine treat. It can be almost impossible to perceive this distraction as a bad thing, and so whatever you were previously focused on is quickly forgotten.

When talking about distractions, interruptions, and temptations, you could be forgiven for thinking that it's all an epic moral struggle—but sometimes it's nothing more than being curious about something else that is happening in your attentional field. You check your phone to see what the ping was, you keep scrolling because you're curious to see what else you may find, and you turn your gaze toward a flashing screen because maybe there is something interesting and relevant there for you to pay attention to. This is not a question of ethics or character, but rather a simple **hijacking of your *natural curiosity* to engage with and learn about the world around you**.

And so, we arrive at a point where curiosity and focus seem to be at odds. If we hope to pay attention, that means reining in our deep curiosity about all those new and potentially interesting distractions happening out there .. . right?

Well, maybe not. Bu first, to get a good handle on how we can work *with* our human nature rather than against it, we need to understand how the attentional field actually works. This field is essentially your internal arena where all your thoughts, feelings, sensations, and perceptions compete for your brain's most important (and limited!) resource: attention.

When you are focusing on something, your prefrontal cortex is activated, and when something else comes along to distract your attention, your parietal cortex is activated. The prefrontal cortex emits slower electrical pulse frequencies than the parietal cortex, which means that the latter is always quicker to respond to stimuli.

In evolutionary terms, it makes sense that the brain works this way; it needs to prioritize novel stimuli in the environment in case these represent threats or time-sensitive opportunities that demand a swift response. In the modern world, paying attention to smartphone pings and flashing screens has no survival advantage at all (in fact, perhaps the opposite), and yet our neurobiology responds in the only way it knows how.

The natural world only prompts our curiosity occasionally and in ways that genuinely connect to threat and danger; the manmade world, however, is rich in never-ending stimuli that harness our attention in order to . . . well, sell things, usually! Now, all of this is to say that if you feel like paying attention is sometimes a major struggle, you are not alone, and you are not to blame.

One way around this problem is to recognize that if we're built for curiosity, we might as well harness and use that tendency, rather than continually burn out trying to push against it. **Intentional curiosity is deploying our attention in a deliberate, conscious, and purposeful way.**

How do you do *that*?

Get Rid of the Obvious, Avoidable Distractions

No willpower is required to resist a temptation that isn't physically allowed to interrupt you in the first place. Go for the low-hanging fruit first and do what you can ahead of time to remove any potential distractions from your workspace. Install blocking apps when you're feeling strong and focused, rather than hoping you'll behave with discipline *after* the pop-up or notification has already seized your brain.

Other things you can do to make distractions less likely:

- Wear a pair of noise-canceling headphones as you work.
- Put your phone in another room, or at least silence it and turn the screen to face downward.
- Put a do-not-disturb sign on the door, lock the door, or go somewhere private where you won't be found.
- Make sure that you are not overly hungry, thirsty, tired, or cold when you sit down to work—don't allow any physical discomfort to distract you.

Increase Your Attentional Load

This one is counterintuitive: Try to actually increase the amount of mental stimulus you are taking in, but only slightly. The "coffee shop effect" speaks to the power of low-level background noise to paradoxically increase focus.

The idea is that you are so completely maxing out your cognitive bandwidth that you reduce your ability to divert attention to a disruption. Think of it as a constant but very minor background distraction that makes it harder to engage bigger, more serious distractions. Experiment a little with what works for you— many people find that unobtrusive instrumental music playing quietly in the background makes it easier to ignore bigger disruptions.

Monitor Your Mind

When distractions arise, try to understand *why* they capture your attention. Your attention may be almost instantly captured by a diversion, but you can choose what you do in the very moment that follows. Is this something *genuinely* important? Random stimuli can snag your attention, but it's you who decides whether it keeps that attention.

Consciously claim your ability, in that moment, to direct and funnel your attention as you see fit. If something truly important and useful has emerged, but you're busy, then take note of it so you can return to it later (assuming the distraction is not a fire alarm, of course).

If you are spontaneously finding yourself with an urge to abandon your task and browse the internet, stare into space, or "check your phone," then rather than just brushing the impulse off, ask if there's anything to learn from it. Could it be time for a break or a recap? Have you gotten stuck in a rut cognitively?

Make Space for Daydreaming

Nothing in life—your brain, your body—is meant to function at full capacity indefinitely.

Breaks are necessary. They are not a distraction from productive action, but a part of the process that allows and supports it. If we continually ignore signals that we are depleted, we may find ourselves growing more distractable—and then we waste more and more energy trying to rein in flagging attention with diminishing returns.

Rest and breaks are essential. Allow your brain to disengage, wander, loosen, and meander aimlessly now and again. Your brain is not just a machine, and thinking is not purely linear; rather, make space occasionally for undirected, free-form play, creativity, and "conscious distraction."

Where does your mind go to when it's let loose? Jot down intriguing ideas and questions that pique your interest, doodle and scribble, or entertain outlandish ideas just for the fun of it. Your curiosity, after all, is a gift and useful instinct—give it free rein now and then so it can serve its natural purpose.

Be aware of all the ways that your environment may be taking advantage of your innate curiosity, and reclaim that by being intentional and focused on what you invest your attention in. Cherish interest in new topics and allow your mind to probe things that capture your imagination and spur your creativity; at the same time, ruthlessly guard against anything seeking to hijack and distort that curiosity.

ACTION STEPS: Make a note today of a few things that you have genuinely felt curious about lately. Set aside some time to indulge your curiosity, or perhaps even use some free-form play time as a reward for completing today's tasks.

The Action Formula

In this section: A neat way to think about the process of intentional action, and how it relates to thoughts, feelings, and physical capacity.

For those who don't consider themselves mathematically inclined, a "formula" can seem daunting and unnecessary. However, the action formula we explore in this section is really just a way to quickly and simply summarize bigger ideas.

The action formula looks like this:

$A = S(T + F)$

How should we read this equation? Each variable is as follows:

A is for **action**, which is the outcome or effect of all the actions taken toward achieving a particular goal.

S is for **stamina** and represents both the mental and physical resources you have available to take the action necessary for your goal. This can be understood as a measure of overall fitness and endurance, not just physically but also cognitively. When you feel physically weak or tired and mentally exhausted, then your overall stamina variable is low, and this will reduce your action.

T is for **thoughts**, which stands for the inner psychological or cognitive processes, beliefs, perceptions, attitudes, thought patterns, and perspectives that all have an impact on your action. Positive and adaptive thoughts have a mathematically larger value, while negative and limiting thoughts have a smaller or even negative value.

F is for **feelings**, which refers, of course, to all the emotions that go toward sustaining or hindering action. Here, emotion is also said to encompass things like desire, passion, motivation, excitement, anticipation, determination, hope, and investment (more positive, greater-value emotions) as well as fear, anger, or doubt (negative, lower value).

Reading the equation through, we can say that **action is the product of your physical capacity and the sum of your thoughts and feelings**.

Throughout this book, we've focused at various points on certain cognitive obstacles, emotional roadblocks, and practical factors that may help or hinder our ability to act well. This equation captures *all* these factors in one place and helps you see their relationship.

At a glance we can see that having a high value for just one of these variables is not enough. For example, we could have extremely positive thought patterns and plentiful good feelings about taking action (T + F), but if we are physically unwell, tired, or uncomfortable, we will still drastically reduce our total action. Likewise, we may be fit, healthy, and full of energy and yet feel completely unable to take action—because our negative thoughts and feelings are undermining us.

The action formula also helps us understand that the drive to act doesn't just come from nowhere or from some abstract sense of willpower. **Action, then, is a visible manifestation of correctly aligned physical, mental, and emotional strength and well-being.**

Why can some people push on with rock-solid persistence and strength, whereas others flake out at the first sign of difficulty? Yes, their attitude matters, but that is closely connected to the way they are seeing and thinking about the situation, and none of it comes into being unless their body—their muscle fibers and the literal nerves in their brain—are in good condition and working to serve that higher goal.

Thoughts and feelings can be considered a determiner of your action, while stamina (or more honestly, a lack of it) is a kind of limiting variable. We are frequently told that if you believe it, you can achieve it . . . but somehow that doesn't seem true when we're hungover, sleep-deprived, or battling an infection! **The game of action is played mostly in the mind—but not entirely.** The body, too, needs to be able to support the action determined by thoughts and feelings.

How can we use this formula to improve our own lives and increase the chance of beneficial action? The same way we work any formula— to change the left-hand side, we change the right-hand side. By increasing the quality of our thoughts, feelings, *and* physical well-being, we increase action.

Thoughts are like the seeds of action, emotions are like the water that nourishes them, and our physical stamina is the actual material of life— the soil in which we cultivate that growing seed. Action is the final result of all our efforts, the fruit of our goal accomplished.

Be Clear on Your Goal and What Action You Are Trying to Achieve

The formula applies to a specific and clearly delineated intention or goal. This is where focus and priorities come in—not every thought or feeling connects meaningfully to every action. We have a certain amount of bodily resources, but we need to be mindful of how we "spend" that on different goals.

What is your goal? Write a book, lose twenty pounds, learn to drive a forklift, make one hundred thousand dollars, or master the accordion? Whatever it is, be clear about the what, why, when, and how. That means knowing what your goal looks like when expressed as action. Next, be honest and take stock of your physical reserves and capacity to carry this goal out. Don't assume that only physical goals take physical energy—the brain is a part of the body, and it uses up physiological resources just the same as any other part of you! What are your energy levels like? How resilience, healthy, and alert are you?

Proactively Manage Your Thoughts and Feelings

At first, you'll need to become aware of what your thoughts and feelings currently are— many of us are not even sure ourselves what we think and feel until we pause long enough to notice.

Try to think beyond just "positive" or "negative" thoughts and emotions, and instead consider them in terms of whether they support or hamper action. "I can do anything" may sound "positive," for example, but its effect on you may be to reduce the likelihood of you taking action (because it triggers pressure and perfectionist thinking). So, rather than considering thoughts and feelings in isolation, look at them in context and become curious about the *function* they are serving in your life. Are they helping you act toward your goals or not?

Naturally, the next step is to gently start shifting all those thoughts and feelings that are not helping or are even getting in the way. Ask yourself: What thoughts and feelings would I have to cultivate in order to make action toward my goal more likely?

Working backward this way gives you something to focus on and work toward. It's not a question of completely reprogramming your brain; just focus on what *is* working and channel more of your energy and attention toward that. If you discover that you actually do possess some super-useful thoughts and feelings, lean into those and find creative ways to amplify them.

Reflect, Adjust, and Celebrate as You Go

The equation is not a law set in stone, but an expression of a dynamic and ongoing relationship between variables. It will change day to day. You can use the formula to help you offset aspects of the equation that may occasionally fall short.

For example, if you know you are having trouble with negative feelings like fear, you might prepare for a tricky task by making sure that you are as well-rested and healthy as possible (increase S), and that you do as much as you can to support positive thinking (increase T). In this way, the total value for A may still be high and you can act anyway, despite your fear.

If you regularly reflect on your process and how the balance of variables is falling day to day, then you can intelligently adjust as you go along. When you succeed, pay close attention to what worked and why, and vice versa. When you take action and achieve your goal, stop and celebrate the fact. You may need to readjust the relevant thoughts and feelings to match your next goal. What matters is that you are staying focused, flexible, and committed to consistent action no matter what.

ACTION STEP: Take a look at the formula and ask yourself, "What variable in the formula is lowest right now?" Take one small step to boosting that.

The Right Kind of Comparison

In this section: Comparison may be the thief of joy . . . but not if you do it right.

Comparing ourselves unfavorably to others is rightly seen as an unhealthy habit that only makes us feel bad. However, **comparison in itself is not negative and can in fact help us be better and inspire meaningful action.**

Consider two people: Person A and B both attend a glitzy work conference. There are plenty of accomplished and rather intimidating people there, and Person A and B, though equally qualified, find themselves having very different experiences.

Person A says, "Oh no, look at all these fake showoffs. They think they're so much better than us, with their stupid clipboards and name tags. I can't believe they get paid what they do, considering they haven't had *that* much more training than we have. Shall we hit the bar?"

Person B says, "Oh, wow, look at all these cool people! How did they get where they are? If they can do it, maybe I can too. I thought I knew a lot, but it turns out there's so much I still need to learn. Do you think I can get one of them to mentor me? When this conference ends, I want to up my game and sign up for a course or something!"

Both Person A and B are making use of comparison, but in very different ways. **Healthy comparison is about viewing other people's success as a source of inspiration and information** rather than as a threat or a statement on your own value or accomplishments. It's the ability to celebrate others' accomplishments and realize that their achievement does not negate your own.

How do we know if we are partaking in healthy or unhealthy comparison? That's easy: Healthy comparison makes beneficial and inspired action more likely, not less.

A person prone to unhealthy comparison, on the other hand, will waste time with blame and excuses, will envy and judge others, and will ultimately do less toward their goals rather than more. It's a question of focus: We can choose to let other people's success fuel our own potential learning and improvement, or we can choose to make it about our failures, inadequacies, or worse, about *their* failures and inadequacies!

Any time you find yourself thinking or saying, "People are better than me," it's a red flag that you may be engaging in unhealthy negative comparisons. After all, people are not better than you on an individual level; it may be true that they know more, have greater skills, possess more experience, or are simply further along in the journey than you are. **But it does not mean that they are innately more worthy or important than you.**

Comparison can be a tool we use to learn and grow, or it can become a stick we use to beat ourselves up with—the mindset behind it matters.

Social comparisons—especially when they're based on superficial things like salary or physical appearance—can lead to low confidence, anxiety, and a reluctance to take risks or voice our opinion. For fear of never measuring up to others, we may fail to act, shy away from challenges, or play small. The irony is that all of this is precisely what keeps us from growing and achieving!

But there's more. Comparisons also lower our empathy and make us judgmental and even bitter or jealous. If we fail to appreciate the hard work and struggle behind other people's success, we may start to develop inaccurate expectations that interfere with our own ability to work hard. Our perspective grows distorted, and we may slip into a kind of victim mindset where we unconsciously set ourselves apart from the success we say we want.

The solution is not to stop making comparisons, but to **use comparison wisely** and in your own best interests. Wrongly dwelling on someone else's good fortune or purely external factors is a bad idea for one obvious reason: It doesn't get us anywhere. Admiring someone's genuine hard work (and not just the external manifestation of that work) is more useful because it supplies us with information that we can act on. *How* did they achieve what they did? How can you do the same? People who are "better than you," then, are merely mentors in disguise.

Don't compare yourself to people who are less accomplished than yourself in order to feel better. It may work for a while, but bear in mind it comes with an opportunity to cost and will only lull you into overconfidence, complacency, and a false sense of your own achievement.

Compare yourself to others who are where you want to be. Compare yourself strategically and from a position of strength. Know that deep down you are not comparing *yourself*, but rather your actions, your strategy, your knowledge, and your skill. All of these things can change—and they will if you embrace opportunities to learn.

Here are some ideas to use comparison to your own advantage.

Rethink Success and Shift Your Perspective

It's important to change the way you see other people's achievements. Realize that success is not a zero-sum game, and them living their best life doesn't take a single thing away from your life or your ability to make it what you want.

When you are internally motivated, other people's actions simply cannot be a threat. If they make you feel insecure or hyperaware of your own shortcomings, then be grateful—this is a reminder of your own unfulfilled potential and perhaps an unmet desire in yourself. It's not always comfortable, but envy of others can sometimes point to a feeling deep down that we are not working as hard as we know we can or toward the things we really value. Pull your focus from them and put it back on yourself and your dreams.

Compare Yourself to Those Who Are Only a Little Ahead

If you're an aspiring singer, for example, you may only demoralize yourself making comparisons against world-famous musicians.

Though their stories can certainly be inspiring, you may be more encouraged by looking at those who are only a few steps beyond where you are now.

There may be a singer in your area who is having plenty of success with local gigs in restaurants, or who has just signed with a small label. How did they do it? How can you do the same thing? The difference, again, is action. Comparing yourself to billionaires and superstars is less likely to give you *actionable* insights than comparing yourself to people who are only a year or so ahead of you on the path.

Compare Insides, Not Outsides

Unhealthy comparison focuses heavily on appearances. Social media in particular specializes in the "highlights reel" of people's lives, offering a glossy but two-dimensional view of their world. These images are end products—and heavily stylized ones, at that. They tell you nothing of the mindset of the person involved, the work they've done, and their approach and strategy. In comparing yourself to them, you are none the wiser on what actionable steps to take to reach that dream.

A far more useful form of comparison is to pay attention to people's "insides"—namely, their attitudes to work and life, their values, their mindsets, their daily habits, their lifestyle, their work ethic, and the way they deal with adversity.

These things, after all, give you real clues about how you can be like them. Be realistic and strategic. Instead of admiring people who *look* good as they cross the finish line, compare yourself to people who actually put in the work to train for the marathon, and become curious about their methods . . . which may be far less glamorous!

ACTION STEP: Pick someone who you feel a little intimidated by, or even badly envious of. Try to turn that envy into admiration and inspiration. They are your potential mentors and role models! What is one action they do every day in their own lives, and can you do a similar action yourself?

Bright and Dark Spot Analysis

In this section: Why it's okay to have ups and downs—and how both positive and negative "deviance analysis" can be used to your advantage.

If you have been applying some of the concepts shared in this book so far and have been doing so consistently for any length of time, then you will start to notice something: Sometimes

173

you'll do really well . . . and other times you'll fall annoyingly short of what you know you're capable of.

When it comes to building resilient, adaptive, and realistic *lifelong* habits of action, however, **we need not fear this rise and fall pattern— because we can use it to our advantage**. When we start to work from an action-oriented point of view and consistently favor a growth mindset, we focus on process and not outcome. That means that everything we do— the successes, the failures, and everything in between—is just grist for the mill.

Managers sometimes do what is called a "bright spot analysis," which is just a fancy way of talking about the peaks and high points of your experience. Though it's usually applied in a work context, we can use the principle in our personal lives, too. By paying close attention to what works, we can empower ourselves to find out exactly *why* it works so we can replicate it.

Now that we are nearing the end of the book, in fact, you can do a bright spot analysis on your own experience as you moved through each section. Not every chapter would have resonated with you, and not every technique or concept would have suited your life. But if you know what did make a difference, then you can learn how to do more of it. Thinking back now to the book but also to your own projects and tasks from the preceding week, ask yourself the following:

- Which day was your most productive? Most enjoyable? Most meaningful?
- What was the single most impactful thing you did?
- Which relationship or connection has proved most fruitful or valuable?
- Which technique or idea has impacted you most?
- When did you feel most inspired and energized—what were you doing?
- What actions or choices did you make that you were particularly proud of?

By asking these questions, you are zooming in on your personal bright spots. Next, take things further by identifying the *root cause* of this bright spot.

- What exactly made it so bright?
- What came immediately before?
- What allowed it to take place?
- In what ways was this bright spot different from everything else?

Once you have isolated exactly what it is that has produced the bright spot, you are in the position to *recreate* that deliberately by bringing about the root cause again. Ask yourself,

- What you did then, is there a way to do it every day or at least more often?
- If a particular relationship is going well, can you approach other relationships in a similar way? What behaviors can you carry to other people or situations?
- How can you bring more of the same into your day-to-day activities?
- What do you need to do to make the root cause easier or more likely next time around?

So, to summarize, the process is simple:

Monitor your behavior over a certain tie period and **pick out the best**, brightest, most productive moments.

Next, **identify the root cause** behind this bright spot. There may be several.

Finally, try to **reproduce the root cause** if you can. Take note if it works, and adjust accordingly.

Here's an example:

You notice that you had an especially enjoyable and productive morning last Wednesday when you woke up and easily completed several hours of deep work without difficulty. You achieved more than you managed in the rest of the week combined. Why? You break down all the events leading up to the morning and discover that you actually had a great sleep the night before.

But *why* did you sleep so well? You realize that on that Tuesday evening you didn't watch TV—instead you played board games by candlelight and went to bed thirty minutes earlier because of a power cut. The way forward is obvious: Try every day for the next week to go to bed thirty minutes earlier and to not watch TV before bed.

Well, that's how we conduct a bright spot analysis or analysis of "positive deviance" from the norm. Does that mean we can also analyze all the times we do especially badly? Yes!

"Dark spot analysis" works on exactly the same principle, and in fact may even be more useful when it comes to making gains and improvements. Ask all the same questions as above, but this time look specifically for the worst day, the least productive moment, the unhappiest relationship, or the most boring, confusing, or low-energy parts of recent memory.

Once you've identified the root cause of this low point, you can again ask, how can I do less of this? How can I make sure that I'm not setting up the same cause again? How can I do the opposite of what I did then?

One interesting thing about bright and dark spot analysis is that you don't even have to go through the experience yourself to derive benefit from it. You can carefully analyze the peaks and troughs of *other people's* lives and pay attention to their causes, and how you can avoid or repeat them. You can conduct such analyses on a long-, medium-, or short-term scale, and in any area of life.

It's a great idea to do one small analysis every day—even tiny changes can add up. Combine this with a broader analysis every week or month so you can observe any larger patterns as they emerge. In some cases, you may even be able to detect causes that are as distant as a year out and make efforts right now to ensure a different outcome for yourself next year.

There is one final step to conducting bright/dark spot analysis in the most effective way possible, and of course it has to do with moving deliberately from analysis to action. **Insight alone is not enough and does not bring about change.** Understanding why a thing happens will not automatically lead to you making the right choice in the future—to do that, you still need to consciously commit to taking action.

That's why once you've identified bright and dark spots and their root causes, you need to set up a concrete and realistic plan of action to create more bright spots. If going to bed thirty minutes earlier is the root cause, then schedule that in, set alarms, and work hard to create a new habit. Keep it up for one or two weeks, then appraise the difference it makes— are you having more super-productive mornings like you did that special Wednesday?

In the same way, if you're doing a dark spot analysis, it may make sense to deliberately plan and schedule an opposing behavior or competing action to start displacing the one that precipitates the dark spot.

It may take you a little while to correctly identify root causes, but that's okay—each iteration and experiment brings you closer. This is what a growth mindset and action-oriented frame of mind looks like in action. It means you don't worry about getting things right or perfect because you know that it's in the *deviations* from perfect that you actually learn the most.

ACTION STEP: Look back on your journaling through all five chapters so far and conduct a bright and dark spot analysis. Remember to complete the process by scheduling inspired action based on what you learn.

Getting Comfortable in the Discomfort Zone

In this chapter: Change never feels especially good—and that's okay!

Sometimes, the unspoken assumption behind the advice given by so many productivity gurus is that if you just find the right routine, establish the right habits, and adopt the right mindset, then you will be forever spared from having to endure any uncomfortable, unpleasant, or confusing feelings in your life. Sadly, it's this unrealistic expectation that leads people to abandon their hard-won gains when things get tough.

Taking action is valuable because it is the only real way we can engage with our world, shaping it (and ourselves) according to our will. When we take action, we also take control, and we put ourselves squarely on the path of learning and improvement. **The thing is, this path is not guaranteed to be easy, fun, or simple!**

Remembering that we want to reorient our mindset toward process (not outcome), we need to deeply internalize the idea that **we are never really *finished*.** When our inspired action has brought about the goal we set our intention on, we celebrate, but the horizon is still there, beckoning us to rise to new challenges that appear. As we grow and change, so do the lessons we need to learn.

We are therefore never in the position of just camping out at the finish line, reveling in our victory with nothing more that we need to learn, and nothing further to be gained. If you think about it, aren't you worthy of something better than that?

You may have heard a thousand times that life begins when you step out of your comfort zone, but it can be a difficult message to *believe* on a deep level. Now, you don't have to enjoy or like discomfort—that's a contradiction. But you do need to make peace with it. Today, there is plenty of muddled thinking around what is and isn't an acceptable level of discomfort in life. Aren't we supposed to be reducing anxiety at all costs? Isn't it a matter of self-love to go easy on ourselves and not do anything that feels scary or awkward or embarrassing?

Well, the unfashionable answer is *no*. **If real change is something you want, then discomfort is non-negotiable**, and sooner or later you will need a conscious strategy for dealing with it. Note here, however, that "dealing with discomfort" does not mean rushing in to *get rid of* that discomfort at all costs. If your current strategy for dealing with discomfort is basically "stop acting" or "avoid the thing that feels uncomfortable," then know that you are choosing the path least likely to end in meaningful change.

If you consistently prioritize ease and comfort, that's what you'll get. But that's *all* you'll get. Discomfort is not a sign that you are doing something wrong or need to stop—in fact it's proof that something is growing and changing in you. The resistance and difficulty you feel is evidence of your active adaptation and learning. It's a good thing.

No tip or trick can help you cheat and avoid inevitable feelings of fear, frustration, boredom, confusion, or fatigue. But with the right attitude, you can face discomfort and realize that it doesn't actually have the power to hurt you. **Discomfort, then, is really not the end of the world and won't kill you.** Failing to act toward goals you value deeply, however, *does* come with risk.

Being prepared to be uncomfortable means being familiar with the process and nature of change. It means knowing that:

- It won't be easy.
- The first time is often difficult and clumsy. Probably the second time, too. In fact, it may be difficult all the way along ...

- You will feel like giving up. It's normal to feel that way.
- You can experience discomfort and still act.
- There is value in doing what you say you will, even if you feel unsure or uncomfortable as you're doing it.
- Being comfortable feels good in the moment, but a life based on comfort alone can lead to stagnation, boredom, low self-esteem, disconnection, self-indulgence, and laziness.
- Often, the thing you've been avoiding contains your greatest opportunity for growth and development.

What does discomfort *mean*? It's not a sign that the universe hates you or that life is unfair. It's not evidence that you should keep your old habits after all. It's simply a growing pain. When you give in and avoid taking action because of discomfort, you are only teaching your unconscious mind that you are smaller and weaker than you are, and that your dreams and goals are not as worthwhile.

Whether your goal is to learn a new skill, overcome a limiting belief or habit, fix a relationship, or completely overhaul your mindset, you will find that **there is only one real "cure" for the discomfort of change: action!**

You don't need to be brave, you don't need to have all the answers, and you don't need perfect confidence or conviction. You just need to act, exactly as you are right now. It really is that simple. Simply refuse to let avoidance be a part of your daily repertoire. In fact, if you are willing to deliberately focus on those things that feel scariest, you can use discomfort as a priceless teacher and guide.

As we near the end of our book, it's worth thinking about the lessons and insights you most want to take from these pages, and how they will look when applied to your life once you finish the final page. Below are some practical exercises to help you reinforce your gains and ensure that you don't lose any momentum when discomfort inevitably rears its head.

Step 1: Identify your discomfort zone

Spend some time identifying the areas and situations of your life that are most likely to cause growth discomfort. Of course, not all discomfort is growth discomfort, but be honest about those uneasy feelings that are standing directly in the way of you working toward your cherished goals. Be as specific as possible—what exactly makes you most uncomfortable and why?

Step 2: Prepare your action statement

Once you've identified the mental, emotional, or physical states you are inclined to shy away from, deliberately set a plan for what you will do instead. For example, if in Step 1 you identified receiving critical feedback from mentors as particularly unpleasant, then you might make a plan as follows: "When I receive critical feedback, I will not dwell on any negative feelings, but instead act in one small way according to the advice I've been given."

Make your own "If . . . then" statements, and make them *before* you face the discomfort. If you wait until the discomfort has already arisen, you may talk yourself out of acting! A good rule of thumb is that action of almost any kind tends to trump anxious rumination, passive dwelling on negative emotions, blame, or self-admonishment. Take a small, active step toward your fear and you instantly diminish its power over you. Avoidance only amplifies fear and discomfort.

Step 3: Ramp it up slowly

Discomfort is a fact of life, but we don't have to be masochists. Start small and dial up your challenge gradually. You are not required to force or punish yourself. Just pick something easy at first and start. Identify something that scares you and do it repeatedly until the sting wears off. Then go a little further. You might only be able to tolerate kind feedback from a close friend at first, for example, but in time you are able to seek out and even enjoy quite frank feedback from complete strangers.

Step 4: Don't take yourself too seriously

When we're feeling afraid of change, our minds can convince us that we're facing an epic life-or-death situation. Things can feel incredibly high-stakes. But all of this evaporates if you can laugh at yourself a little and refuse to take the process too seriously.

Notice yourself complaining internally and coming up with creative excuses, and see the humor in it. When you can affectionately poke fun at these all-too-human tendencies, you take away their ability to derail you. Soon, you can look at your own fear as just a little quirk and know that it has no power to stop you from doing what you know you are capable of.

ACTION STEP: As you complete this book, think about all the things you have already achieved just by choosing to take conscious action toward the things you value. It's time to appraise and celebrate your success, but instead of the outcomes, ask yourself, **"How many times over the course of this book did I act _despite_ my fear, laziness, and discomfort?"** You'll see that the pride and accomplishment you derive from these moments is greater than anything else you could have achieved.

Summary:

- Master your attentional field. Your natural inquisitiveness is a good thing, but steer and direct it into intentional curiosity rather than letting it lead you astray. Intentional curiosity is deploying our attention in a deliberate, conscious, and purposeful way.

- The action formula is A = S (T + F), and it helps us understand the relationship between our physical stamina, our thoughts and our feelings, relative to our ability to take meaningful action. To increase the likelihood of action, we need to support our physical stamina while making our thoughts and feelings as positive as possible. Action comes not from "willpower," but is a visible manifestation of correctly aligned physical, mental, and emotional strength and well-being.

- Comparison can be healthy if you can use it to inspire, motivate, and teach you. Try to learn from others and let their success guide you to take useful action. Be secure in your self-worth and adopt a growth mindset, knowing that the success of others doesn't threaten you.

- Working toward your goals takes time, and there will be ups and downs. Using "deviance analysis" means you can glean useful information from both the bright and the dark spots, seeing what you can learn in both cases.
- Change is uncomfortable and that's normal. Embrace discomfort and make friends with it—it may be your biggest helper.

Made in United States
Troutdale, OR
12/31/2024

27464279R00106